LAND TENURE AND
SOCIAL CHANGE AMONG
THE NYAKYUSA

by

P. H. GULLIVER

(Government Sociologist, Tanganyika)

EAST AFRICAN INSTITUTE OF SOCIAL RESEARCH, KAMPALA, UGANDA

1958

*With gratitude and respect for the anthropological field-work
and writings of Godfrey and Monica Wilson.*

Made and printed in Great Britain by King & Jarrett Ltd., London, S.E.1

CONTENTS

TABLES

SKETCH MAPS

CONTENTS

TABLES

SKETCH MAPS

CHAPTER I

INTRODUCTION

I

In many areas of Eastern Africa the pressure of peasant populations on their tribal lands is a critical feature of the contemporary scene, and this is most especially so in the more fertile parts where the African has accepted the new cash economy and is beginning to appreciate the potentialities of the modern world. The situation has been highlighted recently in the public mind by the publication of the Report of the East African Royal Commission[1] which examined the economic conditions of our time and made general recommendations.

In Tanganyika the overall density of population is low (22 persons per square mile) and the general scale of economic activity still remains little above subsistence level over vast areas of Territory. There are, however, islands of extremely dense populations scattered through the country, often associated with the mountain areas, where soil is fertile, rainfall is reliable and adequate and the cultivation of crops for sale in world markets has gone ahead fairly easily. These populations still comprise peasant farming communities with little capital and their "natural" impulse is to expand their extensive agricultural system rather than to intensify their cultivation on existing holdings. Serious overcrowding soon results for the favourable areas are limited and surrounded by drier bushlands. African attitudes and legal customs concerning their land do not change quickly and they lag behind new conditions of physical limitation and economic development. Whilst the recommendations of the Royal Commission may be valuable in the establishment of general policy, it is obvious that detailed application through time demands a fairly exact knowledge and understanding of particular local conditions if it is to be reasonably successful. This is particularly the case in so large a country as Tanganyika, with its multiplicity of environments and tribal systems of law, land tenure and agriculture, and the social attitudes which encompass them.

The present essay is an attempt, sponsored by Government, to describe and analyse the land and population conditions in one small area of the Territory where a cash economy is emerging and where the pressure of a peasant population on its land resources has become acute. It is hoped that some of this account may be applicable, *mutatis mutandis*, to other similar areas both in Tanganyika and elsewhere, and that the conclusions reached may be helpful in dealing with the problems there; but primarily this is a study of one particular part of the country in order to provide the information upon which detailed policy may be founded.

The Nyakyusa are not entirely typical of many of the Bantu people of East Africa for they have a most distinctive social organisation, peculiar to themselves, based on age-villages and petty, independent chiefdoms. Also, they inhabit a country whose annual rainfall is unusually high, averaging about 100 inches. On the other hand, these people are one of the very few in Tanganyika for whom we have an excellent account of both their pre-European and early European systems of land tenure. Based on this information, obtained *before* modern changes began, we can perceive, analyse

---

1. *East African Royal Commission* 1953-5, *Report:* H.M.S.O. 1955. Cmd. 9475.

and try to understand the nature and reasons for change. Here, then, is a good opportunity for the study of social change – not only in land tenure as such, but also in village and family organisation, political authority and economic life.

II

The Nyakyusa are a Bantu people inhabiting the main part of the Rungwe District in southern Tanganyika, immediately to the north of Lake Nyasa. In 1948 they numbered about 199,000 in that District, but about 10,000 men were probably at the time temporarily absent from their homes and in employment in the mines and towns of the Rhodesias and South Africa (see Gulliver, 1957), whilst about 20,000 had migrated to live in the adjacent Mbeya District to the north.

The tribal area comprises a confined geographical basin surrounding the northern end of Lake Nyasa. It extends only about 40 miles from the tip of the lake at 1,550 feet above sea level to the Poroto Mountains in the north at 8,000 feet; and from east to west is only about 30 miles, from the almost sheer walls of the Livingstone Mountains (with peaks up to 10,000 feet) to the Ndali Highlands (rising to about 7,000 feet). There are therefore unusually large ecological differences within so small an area. Three major regions are to be distinguished: the "Northern Highlands" over about 4,500 feet, the low-lying "Lake Plains" in the south, and the "Central Region" in between. Everywhere rainfall is reliable and high, averaging at least 100 inches annually[1], and this amply compensates for a certain poverty and misuse of the soil, although (and particularly in the Central Region) it brings dangers of soil erosion. Except in the highest parts the banana is the staple food, supported by maize, beans, finger millet and groundnuts. In the Northern Highlands coffee has become well established as the principal cash crop: in the Lake Plains paddy rice cultivation provides both a food and a cash crop: in the Central Region the country is too low generally for coffee and too high and dry for rice; consequently cash-cropping is considerably inferior and the people's standard of living is rather poorer.

The Nyakyusa and their country tended for a long time to be relatively isolated from the outside world by high mountain walls and rain-soaked roads. In addition, or because of it perhaps, they developed an almost unique culture which was supported by considerable conservatism and high insularity. They still continue to regard their African neighbours beyond the mountains as their social and cultural inferiors. The turmoil of the slave-trade in Central Africa passed them by; in modern times they have not enthusiastically accepted Christianity and they have refused to take up the use of Swahili, the Territorial *lingua franca*. In recent years, and most especially since the end of World War II, they have, however, accepted and pushed forward with vigour a rapid and extensive economic development, involving particularly the production of coffee and paddy as cash crops, and large-scale labour migration to the south in the high-wage mining industries. The multiplicity of petty, often tiny, independent chiefdoms has been reorganised to provide four local government areas, each under a Rural Council, in which the old chiefdoms have become something like parishes[2]. Although much of the old conservatism and narrow parochialism persists, yet there is now an atmosphere of accepted change, of a keen desire for economic development, and a general acceptance of a cash economy.

Probably the most significant feature of modern life in the Nyakyusa country is the increasing scarcity of land for agriculture in relation to the

---

1. At Tukuyu, in the Northern Highlands, annual rainfall averaged 99.28 inches between 1919 and 1952: at Kvela, in the Lake Plains, the average between 1940 and 1951 was 106.21 inches.
2. See Kingdon, Z.E.: The initiation of a system of local government by African rural councils in the Rungwe District, Tanganyika; *The Journal of African Administration*, iii, 4, October, 1951.

people's needs. The importance of this can scarcely be overemphasised for a peasant people who are adopting a cash economy and are socially and emotionally deeply attached to their land – their single, continuous source of capital and their tribal heritage. Apart from the possibilities of labour migration which, so far at any rate, are taken up only temporarily and by the younger men, there are no economic opportunities and no capital to compete with the land. In non-economic life the land remains supreme as the persisting basis of society.

As late as 1940 the District Commissioner, Rungwe, was able to write that there was most generally sufficient land for the people's needs in all parts of the country, and the only competition was perhaps in respect of the very best and most fertile tracts, as had always been the case. G. Wilson recorded similar remarks in the late nineteen-thirties. That these observations were correct cannot be doubted. It is known, for instance, that until the post-war years in the Lake Plains – where now land shortage is most acute – there was a broad belt of mainly unoccupied, uncultivated bushland, infested with game, extending from the Livingstone Mountains in the east to the Nyasaland border in the south-west. There were extensive, more or less empty areas in almost every chiefdom. The people were subsistence farmers only, and also banana eaters, and in this well-watered country their agricultural requirements were adequately met on very modest holdings, from most of which two harvests a year could be gathered.

In the brief period of little more than ten years the situation has altered radically to the point of a general shortage of land (except for some parts in the north-west), and especially in the Lake Plains the available land is quite insufficient to meet the demands of the inhabitants. This critical change is the result partly of an increasing population, augmented by some immigration from other tribal areas; but more especially it is the result of the demands for larger arable holdings to meet cash crop aspirations – i.e., money earning. Although both coffee and paddy rice cultivation had begun before 1939, and both were encouraged and developed during the War years, it was not until after 1945 that both of these cash crops became well and generally established and the demand for money incomes became universal.

III

It was in order to investigate this new situation, which was beginning to become serious and to cause concern to Government, that I made a sociological survey in 1955. I had already spent some months in the country in 1954 investigating labour migration in order to provide Government with information and to make recommendations to deal with the problems arising. The second period of work occupied about five months. During both enquiries I was extremely fortunate in having the use of the excellent monographs of G. and M. Wilson who had carried out a conventional anthropological study of the Nyakyusa between 1934 and 1938. Without their basic work behind me, neither of my two studies would have been possible in so brief a time, and I must gratefully acknowledge the real value of their writings.

The intention had been that a complete enquiry should be made into Nyakyusa land conditions in all parts of the country, and that it should culminate in a full recording of tribal land law and custom with a view to its possible reform. In the event only the initial enquiry in the field in the Lake Plains was completed and the results of that alone are described in this essay. Whereas in former days there were probably few distinctive differences between the various parts of the country, in modern times with the introduction of different cash crops, with differential population growths and varying demands on the land, important divergences seem to be arising. For example, in the Northern Highlands there is now a strong tendency for the tight village system to disintegrate as men seek to site their houses, each in his own coffee plot. In the Lake Plains also the structure of the age-village is changing – there the villages persist as such but they come to be inhabited by men of any age and new villages do not emerge with a new chief. No attempt is made here, however, to analyse these variations for they are only now beginning and no satisfactory, detailed information is available for the post-war cash economy of the highland areas.

The Government of Tanganyika has permitted the publication of this essay, and I wish to express my gratitude for its support. The essay is a modified version of my original Report which was presented to Government in January, 1956. The views expressed in it are my own and not those of Government. As usual in my work as Government Sociologist, I have received much valuable assistance, advice and information from officers stationed in the area. The Nyakyusa themselves, as during my first enquiry, were usually cooperative, and at least some of them welcomed my work as a contribution to the easement of their novel difficulties. It would not have been surprising had they remained obdurate and antagonistic towards my enquiries about their land, for like many modern Africans they have a sense of insecurity which is not susceptible to reason. In fact I was able without much difficulty to make any enquiry I wished, to measure sample areas and to discuss the situation in all its aspects. Perhaps it is that an African people welcome a sympathetic enquirer and in their problems genuinely want assistance. The task of a sociologist is of course in some ways rather easier than that of an administrator or technical officer who has to persuade the people actually to accept and practice new ways and to abandon old ways. It is hoped that this essay may be of assistance both to these officers and to the people whom they are attempting to assist and teach.

Finally, I must thank the East African Institute of Social Research which has accepted this essay for publication, and especially Dr. L. A. Fallers who kindly read and criticised the original draft and who drew the two sketch maps.

III

Note: The term, the "Lake Plains", as used in this essay is to be understood to cover the major part of the modern local government area under the Ntebela Rural Council. Omitted are the small groups of Kisi (Ikombe) and Ndali (Ngana) peoples to the extreme east and west respectively. This area contains the alluvial flood plains surrounding the northern tip of Lake Nyasa, and the lowest foothills to the north where the country begins its steep incline towards the Poroto Mountains. To the south lies the lake and to the south-west, beyond the meandering Songwe river, lie the bushlands of the northern part of the Nyasaland Protectorate. To the east are the towering Livingstone Mountains and to the north live the other Nyakyusa groups in the highlands.

The area comprises a fairly compact social and economic region with a common historical tradition. Several of the indigenous chiefdoms stretch across the intermediate boundary between flood plains and foothills. With but one exception the present chiefs are lineal descendants, in their various houses, of the original Mwakyusa who led the people into this lowland area five generations ago. The modern inhabitants are pre-eminently the Nyakyusa-proper.

4

CHAPTER II

THE TRADITIONAL SYSTEM

Although this essay is to be primarily concerned with the modern and changing land and population situation among the Nyakyusa of the Lake Plains, it is quite essential first to have an understanding of the traditional system of political and territorial organisation and of land tenure. This is not mere historicism, for despite changes the traditional system remains as the basis of contemporary land-holding and land law. Whilst actual conditions on the ground change, the Nyakyusa appreciation of those changes and their attitudes to land lag significantly behind. In brief, the traditional system was geared to a situation where there was plenty of land. Today the people find real difficulty in adjusting themselves to a high density of population and an acute shortage of land, with the result that this new situation is aggravated by outmoded practices, attitudes and cultural values.

The ancestors of the present group of peoples now known collectively as the Nyakyusa, moved into the Rungwe region from the Ukinga Highlands to the east beyond the peaks of the Livingstone Mountains. According to legend, which is probably substantially true, these newcomers found a sparsely populated country which they easily occupied. Later, following internecine strife, one group under a man called Mwakyusa left the Masoko area in the centre of present-day Rungwe District and moved down into the Lake Plains. There, probably less than 150 years ago, they drove out the Ngonde people and settled. The sons of Mwakyusa took their shares of the country and people and established their independent chiefdoms. The chiefs in 1956 are the lineal descendants, mainly in the fifth generation, of Mwakyusa, and have a well-known genealogy. The only exception to this occurs amongst the group of tiny chiefdoms in the extreme east under the Livingstones, which now form a single administrative chiefdom under Mwakilasa and number some 400 men. They trace descent from pre-Nyakyusa settlers known as the Saku.

Traditionally, as today, the village was the basic unit both in social life generally and in land-holding in particular. The Nyakyusa village was possibly unique in Africa. It was comprised of men of roughly the same age, together with their wives and young children, and it excluded their fathers and sons and also, very often, their elder and younger brothers. Each village consisted of a close group of houses (often centred on a broad "village street"), with arable and pastoral land around it. Each village had fairly well-defined boundaries with its neighbours. The village was represented as a group and acted corporately through its headman, *lifumu*, who was the guardian of villagers' land rights, the arbiter in land problems and disputes, and the controller of unused land. He was also the political and ritual leader of the village, but nevertheless he was a commoner chosen from amongst the villagers themselves, and was not a member of a chiefly lineage.

Land was owned by the village as a group. Every man resident in the village had a clear right to a site for his house and banana plot and to arable land within the village boundaries; he also had a right to graze his cattle in its communal pastures. Residence gave these rights and members of other villages were excluded. A man who left the village automatically gave up these rights, though if he returned he was able to take up his former holding or its equivalent.

5

Age-villages combined to form a chiefdom under the hereditary chief, *umalafyale,* but active co-operation between villages thus associated was often slight; indeed in the larger chiefdoms there commonly existed intermittent animosity which might break out in raiding or even civil war. The integrity of these larger chiefdoms was weak – for example, when the Nyakyusa were attacked by Sangu and Ngoni war-parties, and later by the Germans, villages of the same chiefdom conspicuously failed to join in common defence. Similarly the land affairs of one village were no concern of any other, and each jealously guarded its own rights.

None of the chiefdoms was large; smallness of scale is typical of Nyakyusa political organisation and social attitudes. In 1955 the smallest indigenous chiefdom contained only 36 men. In 1948 55,700 people were divided amongst about 18 indigenous chiefs, but undoubtedly had not the Colonial Government frozen the system there would have been rather more – at least five more. Today there are 12 recognised "administrative chiefs", amongst whom five have each less than 3,000 people under them, and the largest chiefdom contains fewer than 10,000 people – the average is just over 4,000 people.

Nevertheless the chiefdom, the collection of villages, was important, because in the creation of the chiefdom villages were created, and in its development the villages developed, matured and died away. A village survived only so long as its members lived and by the nature of the age-organisation there was but little possibility of the recruitment of new members, for villagers' sons left to form their own new villages. Their sons eventually came to comprise the core of the new chiefdoms.

In connection with the constitution of a Nyakyusa village and with land tenure, the significant feature of the chiefdom was its establishment, together with the induction of a new chief, at the great "coming-out" ceremony, *ubusoka.* In brief, each chief was succeeded by two of his sons – the eldest son of each of the senior houses of the chief, i.e., of his first two wives. At the "coming-out" ceremony, when the sons were still young men and their father was not a particularly old man, the old chiefdom was divided into two, each part coming under one of the new young chiefs. Before this critical occasion – at which much important ritual was performed – the younger men of the old chiefdom had already moved away from their fathers villages and had established their own incipient villages nearby, each one containing a group of coevals. A Nyakyusa boy from the age of about seven years could not continue to live with his father and mother, but, in company with his equals, built his own hut on a site adjacent to the main village as indicated by the fathers' headman. Until the "coming-out" ceremony these youths' villages came under the control of the old village headmen; but with the induction of the new chiefs they achieved independent status, each with its own headman appointed from among its members by the old headmen. Each new village was allocated a new building site and a new arable area, and quite commonly the old villages, the older men, moved away a little in order to give the younger men adequate access to the land, for it was considered that the young men's needs for land were paramount.

After this wholesale reorganisation of the old chiefdom, when new villages were established and new boundaries demarcated,[1] the old chief himself, the old headmen and the older men (the "fathers") gradually retired from active public life. The old chief was supposed to commit suicide after a time (or was quietly killed off) in order to leave the field clear for his sons; the old headmen became the religious and ritual leaders of the new chiefdoms, with the flavour of elder statesmanship, and the old men's

---

1. 'At the "com'ng out" it is said that "everything is made new", boundaries are redrawn and the new chiefdoms and villages of the young men are ceremonially incorporated'. Wilson, G., 1938, p. 31.

villages grew ever smaller and became extinct as their members gradually died off in old age.

A Nyakyusa village, then, owed its being to this most significant political, social and religious event. Each village had its area approximately demarcated, and each headman was ritually and magically strengthened in order to lead and protect his men and their families.

This particular system operated satisfactorily in the demographic and land-using conditions of the old days. By the process of bifurcation, briefly described above, new chiefdoms and new villages were formed for each generation. Although the population appears to have been increasing rapidly there was always sufficient land to create two chiefdoms where one had existed before, and to create new villages and more villages than had existed before in the old chiefdom. The two new chiefs were able easily to move apart and find sufficient and more than sufficient land for their needs.

The system of bifurcation, the ideal of the Nyakyusa, did not always work out so neatly in practice – at any rate it often did not in the Lake Plains. Sometimes it did work; for example, the present chiefdoms of Lazarus and Koroso are the two parts of their grandfather's single chiefdom, which split up under their respective fathers. Similarly, the present Mwakipesile and Mwamasangula chiefdoms stemmed from a single unit, whilst the Mwaki-pesile chiefdom itself today is really two indigenous chiefdoms, but the Government would recognise only the senior brother's claim to chiefship and allowed him authority over the whole. Even where a single new chiefdom succeeded the old (frequently as the result of civil war in which one brother subjugated the other) the essential dichotomous arrangement persisted so that the resultant single unit had two distinct halves, each with its own head with his villages and headmen. In any case, whether traditional bifurcation occurred or not, and right down to modern times, new villages have been established at the time of the "coming-out" of the new chief. The basic village system showed greater persistence and remained truer to type than did the chiefdom and the wider political system.

The real authority of a Nyakyusa chief was not in general very great, although individuals here and there achieved personal importance. A chief was accorded a great deal of prestige and honour, and by tribute and gifts he frequently became pre-eminently wealthy. He was supposed to be kept informed by his headmen of all important village affairs and to approve all matters concerning the land; but the village headman was in fact the real land authority, who attended to the details of land allocation and land use within his village. A chief could not do this, and in fact only in so far as he had the support and loyalty of his headmen had he any authority at all. "A chief is a chief because he has headmen," one informant put it to me – he was a prominent chief himself. A villager said: "A chief does not own the chiefdom, or the land. We, the people together, own it." A chief could, without notice or advice, take any unoccupied land for the use of himself or of his kinsmen, but he could not allocate it to others; both headman and villagers would have indignantly and successfully protested had he tried, as some occasionally did. Land disputes, an uncommon feature in a country where land was plentiful, were settled by the headman of the village in question; they were the private affairs of the village and the chief had no right of interference. Inter-village disputes first came before a meeting of the headmen concerned, with perhaps the assistance of the senior headman of the chiefdom. Only if a dispute could not be settled and if it seemed likely to threaten general peace within the chiefdom would the disputants go before the chief himself, who even so relied and had to rely heavily on his headmen to secure a settlement. So delicate was his position that he might be unable to resolve inter-village disputes for fear of witchcraft reprisals against him by the unsuccessful party.

Sometimes a chief who was a powerful personality rode roughshod over his headmen and achieved a measure of autocracy; but most headmen would not allow this and in their opposition they had the full support of their villagers, as well as the moral backing of public opinion. There are remembered cases in pre-European days when a chief was deposed or reduced to a non-entity by his headmen acting together in the face of what they considered to be encroachments on the inviolability of village unity and independence. In any case, however, even the strongest chiefs were little disposed to interfere in the land matters of their villages; few wished to be bothered with the details of land rights. A chief could legitimately complain if he were not kept informed by his headmen, but his approval of their actions – and most especially in land matters – was very largely a formality.

Traditional Land Tenure

As already briefly described, a village comes into formal existence at the time of the formation of a new chiefdom. At that time its building site and arable and pastoral areas were roughly demarcated by the retiring headmen of the old chiefdom. Within the village, members were allocated their house plots and each man tended to take the strip of land stretching behind his plot and make his field there. The land was shared out on a friendly, co-operative basis; the new headman smoothed out any difficulties and settled any disputes. Thus was the pattern of land-holding established. Apart from the relative value of a plot proximate to a man's house, there was little or no cause for dispute as land needs were small and the supply plentiful. An established villager could, without notification or special permission, extend his cultivation to any land which lay vacant – i.e., which was not in use or under fallow by a fellow-villager. There was therefore no need for a man to try at first to grab more land than he immediately required, nor did he need to be jealous of his neighbours' claims.

A villager's rights to the use of his land were quite secure and he had no fear of eviction or of the seizure of part of his holding. It is said that very occasionally a chief might take a man's holding but I think, at least in the Lake Plains, that this must have been most unusual. In fact, of course, so long as a man was allowed to reap his crop there was little value attached to the plot as such when nearly similar ground stood unused. Men sought security not on their plots of land, but in their membership of the village community, which assured them of their continuing rights to adequate opportunity for cultivation over the years. However, virtually every man had an excellent security of tenure on his holding during the mature life of his age-village (i.e. until at least the next "coming-out" ceremony), and if he died his heir, should he wish, could come and live in his house and cultivate his fields without hindrance. The way in which he cultivated, though of course strongly conditioned by custom and convention, was his own affair, and he sub-divided his holding amongst his own family as he thought fit. He could not, however, allocate any of his land to a man living in another village, nor could he permit it to be cultivated by such a stranger.

Through fear of witchcraft, because of persistent illness, misfortune or unfriendliness, in order to live near a relative or friend, or to inherit elsewhere, a man might leave his village and his age-mates. Then he had to give up his land-holding. When a man moved because of witchcraft or illness (much the same thing and a chief cause of movement) his land was normally left idle pending his hoped-for return, and his former neighbours would do all they could to induce him to return to his old home and fields – even to the use of force (see Wilson, G. 1938, pp. 32-3). His departure was an accusation against them, and a disturbance of co-operative unity. If the man consistently refused to return, or if it was known that he had definitely left for good, his

8

land automatically reverted to the common pool. An established villager might decide to use part of it perhaps, but not before prudently gaining the approval of the headman, lest the migrant return later and accuse him of unlawful and unfriendly seizure. If the headman agreed, as he would after a time in most cases, the newly acquired plot became part of that villager's holding with as secure a title as the rest. Such vacated land could also be allocated by the headman to a newcomer or, before the sons' village was established, to the son of a villager.

If a man had more land than he could cultivate – because, for example, his sons had left him to cultivate in their own villages, or his wife had died – he was under no essential obligation to give up any part. The headman might, if the need arose, try to persuade him to release a portion in order to make it available to someone in need; but the land-holder could refuse and the headman had to accept his refusal. As a chief depended on the support of his headmen, so did a headman's position ultimately depend upon at least the passive support of his villagers, from whose ranks he was chosen.

At the next "coming-out" ceremony the men of a village of the old chiefdom might be required to move aside in order to allow the young men, their sons, to take up the better building sites and farming land. This they traditionally did voluntarily and they built new homesteads on one side and cleared new arable plots. Once re-established in this manner, these older men would not be disturbed again and they remained secure in their new holdings. How often in fact such a displacement took place I cannot say, but it certainly seems to have occurred sometimes, for one can still trace old village sites which appear to bear out the common Nyakyusa story.

In all this it must be remembered that the spirit of village unity and coevality was held in far higher esteem than land in such a fertile country where land was plentiful and subsistence farming required but small-sized holdings. Security of tenure and defined rights to particular plots are notions belonging to a different situation and age; when land begins to be scarce and to have an economic value, and when there is danger of men not being able to obtain as much as they need roughly where they need it.

Newcomers were invariably welcomed to a village: they were supplied with a house site and an arable holding and were assisted with food until the first harvest. They were an addition to the numerical size and physical strength of the village, and they increased a headman's prestige. Their rights were no less assured than those of founder-members of the village, although their social position was less secure, at least at first, for they had not shared in the history of the community and had not grown up with the ties of village association and comradeship amounting almost to kinship.

Traditional rights in trees may be mentioned briefly. Trees were in- herited without difficulty along with the land on which they stood, and a brother or son would commonly inherit the deceased's valuable trees without bothering to take the arable land around. If a man left his village and thus forfeited his land there, the position was different. Banana trees went with the land and a new occupant simply took them over; bananas are of no great value as they grow so readily and ubiquitously. Bamboos are more valuable (being used extensively in house-building) and any left behind in this way could be claimed in the first instance not by the village but by the chief. If the chief wanted them they became his property, or he could grant them to any man he favoured. Usually a chief was content to leave them: then the local kinsmen of the departed man had first claim, and if they had no use for them, or if no kinsmen were resident in the village, they became village property to be allocated by the headman. *Usyunguti* trees[1] were regarded in

---

1. These are valued oil-bearing trees planted by the Nyakyusa of the Lake Plains, the botanical name of which I do not know.

the same way as bananas, to be allocated along with the vacant surrounding land, although sometimes it seems that a chief might successfully lay claim to them. Trees supplying firewood were generally plentiful in the surrounding bushland. A man would not cut wood on another's holding, and standing trees merely went with the land if it was taken up by anyone else, in the same way as useful stands of thatching grass did.

In conclusion of this summary account the following points may be reiterated as important to the understanding of the traditional system:—

(i) Land was plentiful in relation to the people's needs and extensive areas were left untouched.

(ii) Land was owned by the village as a group, acting under its own headman, who was the arbiter and the allocator of fields.

(iii) Land was held in usufructory right only by a resident member of the village, and every resident had the right to a house and banana-grove site, to sufficient arable land and to the use of communal pastures and woodland.

(iv) The individual's security of tenure was good, in so far as this was thought at all important.

(v) The power of the chief was slight in land matters; he had no authority to allocate land.

(vi) Other villages, whether of the same chiefdom or not, had no claim in, or authority over, a village's land and land affairs.

CHAPTER III

CHANGING CONDITIONS AND THE PRESENT SITUATION

Population

At the African Census in 1948 there were recorded, in their own tribal area, approximately 198,000 Nyakyusa at an average density over the land available for their use of 212 persons per square mile.

In the Lake Plains alone there were, in 1948, 55,700 inhabitants living at an average density of 268 persons per square mile. Population densities in the other Nyakyusa areas were rather lower than this.

These figures do not, however, give the full picture from the point of view of land occupation and use, for large numbers of men, and some women, were at the time of the Census absent from their homes and living temporarily in employment areas abroad – chiefly in the Rhodesias and South Africa. I have estimated elsewhere that approximately 8,000 men would have been away in 1948, of whom 95 per cent. or even more would return to settle down at home, for there was only a very small proportion of men who remained more or less permanently absent. That is to say, these men remained dependent for their land needs on their own tribal territory, and indeed at least some were active land-holders whilst the rest had lesser rights in family holdings.

If, therefore, we include these temporary absentees, the measure of the pressure of population on the land is shown by an average density of population for all Nyakyusa of 220 persons per square mile. At least 3,000 of these migrant labourers (possibly more) had their homes in the Lake Plains, and this number increased the density of population dependent on the land resources of this region to 282 persons per square mile.

The statistically average family in 1948 comprised about five people, and therefore the population density can be restated in the form that for all Nyakyusa there were available about 15 acres of land per family. In the Lake Plains there were about 12 acres of land available. These averages do not, of course, take account of either unusable land such as swamps, steep slopes, infertile tracts, etc., nor of the land necessarily taken up by roads and paths, open spaces in the villages and the like.[1]

These figures indicate that, taking a broad and general view based on averages, the density of Nyakyusa population or their pressure on their tribal lands ranked amongst the highest in Tanganyika in 1948.[2]

Unfortunately census enumerations before 1948 were too unreliable to allow of any satisfactory estimate of the probable rates of population increase, but from general information and internal evidence it is thought not unreasonable to suggest that in the Lake Plains population is increasing perhaps at the rate of one per cent. per annum; and in the rest of the tribal area the annual increase may be one and a half per cent. per annum. The high incidence of malaria and other debilitating diseases in the Lake Plains during the flood period of the wet season each year accounts for the lower estimate of increase there.

---

1. No account is taken in these calculations of Nyakyusa who were permanently resident in others parts of the Territory. They lived chiefly in Mbeya District (Unyiha, Usafwa and Mbeya Town) where they numbered about 20,000 in 1948.

2. The higher population densities in 1948 were as follows:—Ukara Island (Ukerewe District) 500, Moshi 257, Ukerewe 208, Lushoto 170, Rungwe (including Nyakyusa, Ndali, Lambia, Kisi, etc.,) 161, Mwanza 160, Arusha 154, Kwimba 140. Figures extracted from *Population Density*, Govt. of Tanganyika, 1955.

If therefore, pending the next Census to be made in 1957, we assume these rates of increase, then by 1955 it may be estimated that the Nyakyusa numbered about 217,000 at an average density of 233 persons per square mile, allowing 13.7 acres of land per family of five. For the Lake Plains alone, the population in 1955 would have been nearly 60,000 at an average density of 287 persons per square mile, with 11.2 acres per family. If we also include the estimated number of absentee migrant labourers in the base year of 1948, then there were in 1955 perhaps 63,000 people dependent on the land resources of the Lake Plains at an average density of 303 per square mile, though in fact some 6,000 men were temporarily absent from home in that year.

The figures and estimates are given in Table I. These averages do, of course, hide some considerable and significant local variations which are further described at pages 14 ff. below.

TABLE I
NYAKYUSA POPULATION

	1948 Census			1955 Estimates		
	a	b	c	a	b	c
Lake Plains at increase of 1% p.a.	55,700	268	11.9	59,700	287	11.2
Central Region at increase of 1½% p.a.	48,500	224	14.2	53,800	248	12.9
N.E. Highlands at increase of 1½% p.a.	40,300	183	17.4	44,700	203	15.8
N.W. Highlands at increase of 1½% p.a.	53,200	185	17.3	59,000	205	15.6
NYAKYUSA in tribal area	197,700	212	15.2	217,200	233	13.7

a = population
b = persons per square mile on land available for African use.
c = average acreage available per family of 5 persons.

Assuming that there were in 1948 about 3,000 men temporarily absent from their homes in the Lake Plains but who remained dependent on the land resources of that region, then the following estimate may be made:–
Lake Plains – persons resident at home and temporarily abroad:–

a	b	c	a	b	c
58,700	282	11.3	62,935	303	10.6

The approximate areas available for African use in the tribal lands (excluding alienated land, forest reserves and main roads) are:–

Lake Plains – 208 sq. miles   N.E. Highlands – 220 sq. miles
Central Region – 217 sq. miles   N.W. Highlands – 288 sq. miles
BuNyakyusa – 933 sq. miles

In these calculations no account is taken of unusable land such as swamps, steep slopes, thicket, etc.

Cash Cropping: Paddy Cultivation

This condition of a high density of population exists in a modern economy in which cash-cropping is universally accepted and desired. Under the former subsistence agriculture, because of heavy rainfall and natural annual flooding, quite small-sized holdings were adequate to satisfy a family's food requirements. Two harvests a year are easily obtained in some combination of maize, beans, groundnuts and finger millet, with a few small "luxury" crops; and the banana groves yield continuously. The Nyakyusa were and are extremely fortunate in their food supply, and seldom experience shortages such as occasionally or even commonly afflict many peoples of East Africa.

Rice was first introduced in 1896 by two chiefs who obtained the seed from Nyasaland Arabs; and in 1898 the Moravian Mission and a Swahili

12

trader brought in other seed. The trader himself planted a large plot and his success seems to have stimulated the Nyakyusa to follow suit. There was a slow but gradual development of planting and by 1932 it was estimated that some 500 tons of hand-hulled rice were sold. It had become clear that the alluvial flood plains around the northern tip of Lake Nyasa were ideally suited to paddy growing. Until 1942 the people continued to hand-hull their crop and sell the rice, but in that year they were persuaded to sell the paddy direct to a locally established mill. Following initial difficulties in milling, handling and marketing, the Government built a store capable of holding 14,000 bags and it also took over the whole of the marketing with a seconded District Officer in charge. In 1947 the cultivators formed their first co-operative society. This movement has been encouraged by Government and the local Co-operative Union now deals with storage and marketing with the guidance of a Government Co-operative Officer.

The figures of sales of rice and paddy are given in Table II.[1]

Paddy has become a well-established crop, not only as the single cash crop of the region, but also as a food crop second only (or even equal) to the traditionally staple banana. About four-fifths of all arable holdings are paddy fields – though parts of these are used for dry season crops of maize, beans, etc. Virtually every Nyakyusa land-holder now grows paddy, and the vast majority regard it as their main crop. Cultivation is mainly by ox-plough followed by broadcast sowing and hand-weeding. Government efforts to encourage nurseries and planting out in rows have so far been entirely unsuccessful. Yields and perhaps quality too are thought to be lower than need be; the chief factor in production seems to be the degree of natural flooding during the wet season.

TABLE II

SALES OF RICE AND PADDY, 1932-56*

		tons			tons
1932	..	500	1945	..	1,200
1933	..	600	1946	..	2,700
1934	..	600	1947	..	3,300
1935	..	600	1948	..	2,100
1936	..	700	1949	..	3,700
1938	..	700	1950	..	2,300
1939	..	1,200	1951	..	1,200
1940	..	1,500	1952	..	2,000
1941	..	1,600	1953	..	5,700
1942	..	2,200	1954	..	5,900
1943	..	2,800	1955	..	5,700
1944	..	2,900	1956	..	3,000

*1932-41—hand-hulled rice, estimates only.
1942-47—paddy, sold through Government agency.
1948-56—paddy, sold through cultivators' co-operatives.

The cultivation of paddy requires relatively large-sized holdings due to the nature of the crop and the local extensive method of agriculture – for example, to produce a given income requires a far larger area of paddy in the Lake Plains than of coffee in the Northern Highlands of Nyakyusa country. As paddy cultivation became established, men increased their arable holdings in order to earn their money incomes. Larger holdings, rather than improved agricultural techniques, have become directly connected with higher incomes, and so the demand for more land set in. Assisted by the now general use of ploughs, paddy growing increased rapidly wherever it was found ecologically possible – i.e., within the alluvial flood plains and the coterminous area of annual natural flooding. Before this new demand for land emerged there were, even in the most highly populated parts, extensive areas which were more or

---

1. Information has been supplied by the Co-operative Officer, Tukuyu.

less uncultivated. These areas can easily be picked out today by the absence of village sites and banana groves. There was something of a rush to grab land in such areas and in the less densely populated parts of the chiefdoms. Today in my personal experience – for no general survey has been attempted – there remains little or no unused land within the paddy-growing region which can, by native techniques, be brought under the plough; and indeed men are attempting to grow paddy on unsuitably raised land where inundation is inadequate. Communal cattle pastures have shrunk as arable holdings extended until they remain only where cultivation is profitless.

The demand for land has far outrun the physical supply, and in 1955 it still seemed to be insatiable. The initial cycle was that a desire for more money to permit of a higher standard of living created a demand for more land on which to produce more cash crops; but the increased level of income then further stimulated money demands to raise standards higher again, thus bringing a renewed demand for land. The cycle has now been halted by the lack of further land to meet the people's needs, but the demand remains nevertheless and is indeed increased by rising costs of living.

This economic picture is, of course, oversimplified, but it may serve to illustrate the nature of forces at work in the situation. I would not wish to overemphasise the snowball effect, for the bulk of the population remains still largely content with only a little over earlier standards; but increasing numbers of men and their families are coming to seek something better. Bicycles have become something of a general necessity; a variety of good clothing and shoes is considered quite essential. Only a single decade before the Nyakyusa women still generally went about in the traditional nudity, whereas in 1955 they must have ranked among the very best-dressed African women in the Territory. European-type household goods, crockery and utensils are common. The demand for money, that is for a higher standard of living, has also been greatly stimulated by the experiences of the thousands of labour migrants returning from southern towns and mines, and by the cash and goods they bring back with them.[1]

It is not possible for me to attempt to suggest what a desirable acreage would be for a contemporary Nyakyusa, because money demands, crop yields and selling prices change and the desire for higher standards of living also alter as the potentialities of the new cash economy are increasingly understood. In 1954 the approximate average of Sh.200/- per paddy cultivator was earned from perhaps two or three acres of arable land, but an indeterminable amount of the crop was kept back for home food requirements. As will be shown later many men's paddy fields could have been little more than an acre, and many men, specifically young men, had no paddy land at all. Certainly there were few who held what they considered, at a reasonable estimate, to be sufficient land.

This universal cash crop agriculture and the continuing demand for higher standards of living, and therefore for higher money incomes, is the real cause of the new and rather sudden pressure of population on the land. Of course this economic process operates within a situation of relatively dense population and in a peasant community where land is almost the only form of capital and alternative enterprise is small. The gradual increase of population, although probably small, further aggravates the difficult situation.

Arable Holdings

It was not possible to obtain adequate, satisfactory data to allow the calculation of local population densities, and the detailed results of the 1948

---

1. In Gulliver, P. H.: 1957, an estimate of the cash incomes of Nyakyusa in 1954 is given at pp. 51-2. Data on the cash brought back by returning labour migrants are given at p. 55.

POPULATION DENSITY IN THE CHIEFDOMS OF THE LAKE PLAINS, RUNGWE DISTRICT

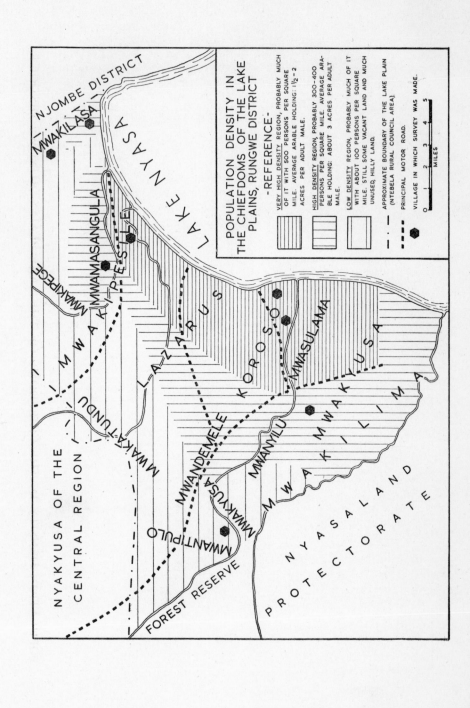

POPULATION DENSITY IN
THE CHIEFDOMS OF THE LAKE
PLAINS, RUNGWE DISTRICT

-REFERENCE-

VERY HIGH DENSITY REGION, PROBABLY MUCH
OF IT WITH 500 PERSONS PER SQUARE
MILE. AVERAGE ARABLE HOLDING: 1½-2
ACRES PER ADULT MALE.

HIGH DENSITY REGION, PROBABLY 300-400
PERSONS PER SQUARE MILE. AVERAGE ARA-
BLE HOLDING: ABOUT 3 ACRES PER ADULT
MALE.

LOW DENSITY REGION, PROBABLY MUCH OF IT
WITH ABOUT 100 PERSONS PER SQUARE
MILE. STILL SOME VACANT LAND AND MUCH
UNUSED, HILLY LAND.

APPROXIMATE BOUNDARY OF THE LAKE PLAIN
(NTEBELA RURAL COUNCIL AREA).

PRINCIPAL MOTOR ROAD.

VILLAGE IN WHICH SURVEY WAS MADE.

0 1 2 3 4 5
MILES

NJOMBE DISTRICT

MWAKILASA

MWAMASANGULA

MWAKIPESILE

MWAKIPEGE

MWAKITUNDU

LAKE NYASA

L-A-Z-A-R-U-S

KOROSO

MWANASULAMA

MWAKYUSA

MWAKILIMA

MWANDEMELE

MWANYILU

MWANTIPULO

MWAKYUSA

FOREST RESERVE

NYAKYUSA OF THE
CENTRAL REGION

NYASALAND

PROTECTORATE

Census have never been issued.[1] However in some sample villages I very roughly measured arable holdings, and my results provide new information even though they can be illustrative only of the modern situation.

In each of the eight villages chosen[2] the arable holdings of *all* the adult male members (whether at home or away at work at the time) of the whole village, or occasionally of a distinct section of it, were measured by the simple and rough method of pacing the borders of every separate plot and converting the resultant figures into yards and thus to acreages. The actual pacing was done entirely by myself in order to try to maintain an even stride on all occasions, but in each village I was well supported by a team of four or five villagers, always including the headman and his assistants. The figures obtained relate only to arable holdings and bear no determinate relation either to crop yields or to non-arable land in the villages concerned. The results are summarised in Table III below.

TABLE III
ARABLE HOLDINGS IN EIGHT VILLAGES

Village and chiefdom	No. of land-holders	Average holding in acres	No. of men holding more than:—		Average size of plots in acres
			5 acres	10 acres	
Kapugi					
Mwamasangula ..	59	3.2	11	1	1
Ikolo Mwakyusa ..	68	3.0	13	0	1.2
Matema Mwakilasa	50	1.9	4	1	0.6
Lugombo Koroso ..	24	1.6	2	0	0.6
Mpunguti					
Mwakipesile ..	63	1.5	1	0	0.5
Kapugi Koroso ..	60	1.3	1	0	0.4
Lusonjo Mwakilasa	12	1.3	0	0	0.6
Busoka Mwantipulo	36	1.0	0	0	0.4
	372 men		32 men (8.6%)	2 men	

From this Table it can be seen that in the chiefdoms of Koroso and Mwakipesile, *in the villages concerned*, the average holding per man was about one and a half acres – and my impression was that in the southern parts of Lazarus's chiefdom and elsewhere immediately surrounding the lake shore similar conditions existed. It may be noted too that in these cases there were large numbers of young men without holdings at all. On the other hand, in the selected villages in the chiefdoms of Mwamasangula and Mwakyusa, the average holdings were about twice as large – three acres; and fewer young men were landless. Note also the cases of the villages in the chiefdoms of Mwantipulo and Mwakilasa in the more northerly parts of the Lake Plains, where the average holdings were one and 1.3 acres respectively, and where yet there was arable land unused and available. In those parts paddy cultivation is very limited because of the higher and hilly country, and the people remain little more than subsistence farmers – perhaps they may be taken as not unlike the traditional, pre-European subsistence cultivators.

Unfortunately I am unable to relate these figues of arable holdings to the total land available in each village, for this would have required survey work beyond my competence. Non-arable land is utilised for village sites with banana groves, roads and paths, pasturage, etc.; but the position is further complicated by varying amounts of unusable land in my sample villages. To give only two examples: within the boundaries of Mpunguti village, Mwakipesile's chiefdom, there are many acres of land adjacent to the Mbaka river which today are unusable because of deep flooding from

---

1. Population figures of any kind are not available even for the separate chiefdoms, let alone for ecological areas.
2. Their approximate locations are indicated on the accompanying sketch-map.

the river in spate during the wet season, although here and there a few plots are cultivated on slightly raised ground. Similarly in Kapugi village, Koroso's chiefdom, some parts are heavily inundated by the Kiwira river. In both these cases flooding has made unusable ground which was cultivated and even built on a generation ago; the degree of annual flooding seems to be decreasing again now so that very slowly a certain amount of new land is becoming available. This cyclical change appears to be directly connected with the long-term rise and fall of the level of Lake Nyasa. On the other hand, in more fortunate villages such as Ikolo, Mwakyusa's chiefdom, and Kapugi, Mwamasangula's chiefdom, there is rather more common pasturage remaining, and village sites, paths, etc., are noticeably less restricted.

The following arithmetical observations may be noted as permitting, perhaps, some guide to population densities in the Lake Plains:–

Persons per sq. mile	Total acreage per family of five	Arable holding per family of five if proportion of total land under arable holdings is:—	
		one-third	two-fifths
300	10.7	3.6	4.3
400	8	2.7	3.2
500	6.4	2.1	2.6
600	5.3	1.8	2.1

(N.B. The statistically average family is composed of five people)

It has been suggested by the Agricultural Field Officer, Tukuyu, that for the whole of Rungwe District perhaps 30 per cent. of all land is under cultivation. He was not prepared to place any reliance on this figure, and certainly for the Lake Plains it must be higher.

To summarise my own tentative conclusions and in order to obtain some kind of picture of the current land situation, I suggest the following division into regions:–

A. The flood plains proper

1. **Very high-density region** – the arable land available under present conditions amounts to about $1\frac{1}{2}$-2 acres per adult male and the local density of population is probably in the region of 500 persons per square mile: – in most of the chiefdoms of Mwasulama, Koroso and Lazarus, the south-eastern part of Mwakipesile's and the eastern part of Mwakyusa's chiefdoms.

2. **High-density region** – there is available about 3 acres of arable land per adult male and the local density of population is between 300 and 400 persons per square mile: – in the chiefdoms of Mwamasangula, Mwanyilu and Mwakilima, the southern part of Mwakilasa's, the centre of Mwakyusa's and much of Mwandemele's chiefdoms.

B. The remainder of the Lake Plains (Ntebela)

3. **Low-density region** – here there remains much vacant land (some usable, some scarcely usable) and population density is probably little over 100 persons per square mile, and even lower than that in the most northerly parts: – the northern, higher areas comprising the north of Mwakyusa's (Mwisula's) chiefdom, the remainder of Mwandemele's, the whole of Mwantipulo's, Mwakatundu's and Mwakipege's chiefdoms, together with the northern part of Mwakipesile's and of Mwakilasa's chiefdoms.

This summary description is, and can be, only very approximate, taking no account of the complexity of local variations to be seen on the ground. It is illustrated in the accompanying sketch-map.

It may be emphasised that in the two high-density regions practically all available land is in use. In the "high-density region" (No. 2 above) it may be possible to reduce slightly the non-productive areas taken up by village sites, but nowhere will this be easy or even desirable, and already most of the vacant spaces between houses are packed with banana groves, small plots of maize, squashes, tobacco, etc., and useful trees (bamboo, citrus, mango, kapok, *usyunguti* and firewood). Artificial drainage would, of course, make more land available along the rivers, but this is in general beyond the abilities and resources of the Nyakyusa without considerable outside assistance.

Finally, in this matter it is to be remembered that in addition to a man's arable holding, each of his wives has a banana plot at her house from which she obtains her staple foodstuff. Such plots amount to perhaps about a tenth of an acre on the average. On the other hand, the Nyakyusa are no longer prepared to tolerate a predominantly banana diet. Rice has, in most areas of the Lake Plains, become almost as important as bananas.

Large-sized Holdings

Some blame for this novel shortage of land and the smallness of the average holding has often been laid upon that minority of Nyakyusa who have exceptionally large holdings, and also upon the immigrants from beyond the Lake Plains who have come to settle there during the past decade.

The occupiers of large-sized holdings are rather fewer than has some-times been supposed. The notoriety of large land-owners, such as some of the modern chiefs with as much as 25-30 acres, has brought more attention to them than is really warranted. Most chiefs and village headmen have arable holdings of above average size, as a result of their privileged positions in the land allocation system and because of their prestige influence; but they remain a small minority and their number is bound to decrease in the future as inheritance causes sub-division of their holdings, for most of them have also more than the average number of wives and sons. In the two high-density regions it is clearly impossible for any man much to increase his present holding. As will be shown later (see page 24) the modern trend is not unnaturally towards a dangerous fragmentation of holdings.

The data obtained in this matter for my eight village samples are summarised in Table III, page 15. In those villages the two men out of 372 who held more than ten acres were a village headman and the father of a chief.[1] There were seven other headmen and one chief as well as some other locally influential men amongst the people covered by my surveys, but none of them held more than ten acres. There are, of course, some commoners amongst the large land-holders; many of them are close relatives of the chief or headman and have thus received preferential treatment. Some, however, are ordinary villagers who were perspicacious enough to see future trends and to obtain land in the early days before most men realised its new value and when vacant areas were still easily available. Such men are tending to become a new, wealthy class, but on the other hand they are particularly susceptible to the begging of kinsmen and friends who have insufficient land. If they are not to be regarded as unneighbourly or even anti-social (perhaps practising witchcraft) they are virtually compelled to be generous sometimes, both with their land and with their profits.

On the whole this minority of men excites little attention or jealousy among the Nyakyusa, who indeed take it for granted that their chiefs and headmen will have more land than ordinary villagers, as befits their status and prestige. If it be thought that by reducing somehow the size and number of these unusually large holdings then the land shortage might be partly relieved, it is a false hope. I scarcely think that the Nyakyusa would welcome any such attempt at interference by administrative action, but in any case it would only provide minor and temporary relief here and there and would not be worth the executive difficulties involved.

---

1. This second man should be a chief himself but he was dismissed by Government on his imprisonment for peculation. He still holds much of the prestige and privilege of a chief for his son is only allowed authority in purely local government affairs.

The Problem of Immigrant Land-holders

Undue importance has also been given to immigrants, but their numbers are relatively small and only significant locally. Since about 1948, or a little earlier, there has been an influx of Africans into the Lake Plains: – Nyakyusa from the Highlands (chiefly from the Central Region – Pakati), Ndali from the Ndali Highlands of Rungwe District and Kinga from the Njombe District to the east beyond the Livingstones; from northern Nyasaland have come Ndali, Lambia and Sukwa, and there are also small numbers of Bemba and others from Northern Rhodesia. They have been attracted in the modern era, when local movement is easier, by the possibility of obtaining land in the northern Lake Plains, where rainfall is so high and untouched bushland has been available.[1]

These immigrants have been and continue to be almost entirely restricted to the north in the "low-density region" (see map, facing page 15). This contained the outstandingly empty area of the country and still there remain vacant lands to be taken up. Such land is usually of relatively inferior quality, easily subject to erosion and loss of fertility on the slopes of the foothills and unsuitable for paddy cultivation except in small, isolated basins. The immigrants, that is, have settled in areas rejected by most Nyakyusa. There, locally, the newcomers outnumber the indigenous population. In the flood plains, the high-density regions, the proportions of foreigners cannot be more than one or two per cent. of the population, and in most villages there are none at all.

It is true that these newcomers do occupy land which might well be used to relieve the congestion nearer to the Lake; but in practice this would not be at all easy. To take a single example: the newly opened area in the north of the chiefdom of Mwakyusa between the Kiwira and Songwe rivers is being rapidly taken up by Ndali from the north-west, Nyasalanders and Nyakyusa from the Central Region (in that order of numerical importance). A few miles to the south, in the centre of the same chiefdom, the inhabitants of the Ikolo area consistently refuse to move although they manifestly cannot meet their land needs within their present villages. They, and others like them, say with some truth that paddy cultivation is less easy and less profitable in these newer and higher areas, and that poor communications make the disposal of produce more difficult. They also say, but more often leave to inference, that they are unwilling to leave their traditional village areas and begin in new parts, even though the move required is only one of a few miles. They have not yet become sufficiently aware of the permanent gravity of modern land shortage to overcome their parochial inertia. By the time they do become aware of it the opportunity may well be lost, for immigrants continue to arrive in twos and threes, and the last vacant land may be taken. To date, however, some vacant lands remain, albeit of poor quality, into which the densely packed Nyakyusa could move, and the immigrants cannot be blamed, at least not yet, for preventing the expansion and resettlement of the local population.

At the moment the chiefs and headmen in these northerly areas are keen to obtain as many of these immigrants as possible in order to swell the number of their commoners, the size of their villages and thus, directly, their own prestige and importance. Newcomers have every opportunity to be allocated as much land as they wish, where they wish, and many are liberally assisted with food in the traditional way until they harvest their first crop. I heard no complaints from either the local Nyakyusa or the immigrants, and relations seemed to be good. Strangers must conform to Nyakyusa ways of life and to the authority of the headman and chief, although

---

1. Immigrants from Nyasaland are said to have come following the introduction of new regulations there prohibiting the cultivation of easily eroded hill areas.

18

in fact they usually settle on the common East African pattern of scattered homesteads, each in its arable area, and not in the tight Nyakyusa village pattern.

I think that the headmen and chiefs concerned would not welcome a restraint on immigration, for it offers them a chance to emulate the numerically produced prestige of their fellows in the flood plains, to whom at the moment they feel inferior. They would, of course, most probably prefer indigenous Nyakyusa, could the latter be persuaded to settle there. As it is, at least some of the Nyakyusa of these northerly villages are trying to move into the flood plains, where they can more easily cultivate paddy and where they can join in a more active and ebullient village life.

One type of foreigner to the Lake Plains is the man (almost invariably a Nyakyusa from the Highlands) who has obtained land but does not settle on it nor in any village. He continues to live in his upland village and comes down to the plains only to cultivate and harvest his paddy field. This is strictly against Nyakyusa land law and custom and, in fact, such an absentee land-holder has often made a substantial monetary gift to the chief or headman for the protection of this extra-legal privilege. These strangers are frequently among the more wealthy upland Nyakyusa, who can afford such payments as these, and often they are of chiefly rank themselves, perhaps having kinship ties with the local chief. There are probably no chiefdoms where such strangers have not obtained paddy fields, though naturally those which contained a good deal of vacant, usable paddy land at the beginning of the cash-cropping era have most.

This does arouse a certain amount of ill-feeling and opposition amongst local villagers who have insufficient land themselves, for they lose land and gain no numerical strength or profit of any kind. The illegal action of the local chief is also condemned, especially as the chiefs should not in any case assume allocatory powers. On the other hand it must be noted that the commoners philosophically accept the supposedly protected prerogatives of their chiefs under European rule and they expect the chiefs to take advantage of them. As with the case of the minority of large land-holders, the actual effect is not particularly great and reformation here would be a minor palliative. Nevertheless in this matter there is a definite and unpopular infringement of villagers' rights and of the local customary law.

One other group of strangers may be noted for the sake of completeness. That is the Kisi, who have for at least two generations been settling along the lake shore itself from Matema in the east to the Songwe river (and beyond) in the south-west. They have come from the north-eastern shores of the lake and in the Nyakyusa area they are principally fishermen who do not, therefore, compete with the indigenous population economically. They cultivate only tiny plots of casava and sometimes of finger millet, although a few of the younger generation are now trying to grow a little paddy also. The total number of Kisi involved cannot be more than a few hundred and they have probably not increased much over the past decades. They follow an almost separate existence from their Nyakyusa neighbours, not inter-marrying, and following their own way of life.[1]

---

1. The main Kisi settlements in Rungwe District are in the Ikombe area, an isolated peninsular south of the Lake Plains, where they number about 1,200. Another 3,000 are scattered on smaller peninsulars and in tiny lakeside basins further south along the Lake shore. They are widely famed as potters, and they exchange their wares for cereal foods to augment their fishing.

CHAPTER IV

THE RESULTS OF LAND SHORTAGE

As indicated in the short outline of traditional land tenure in Chapter II, the system developed and worked adequately in the old situation (both before and after European conquest) when land was plentiful in relation to the people's demands. Any villager who wanted land had the right to be allocated fields: any established villager who wished to expand his cultivation could do so without difficulty. Movement between villages was easy, and especially after the establishment of European peace, for everywhere new-comers were welcomed to increase the strength and prestige of the village, and land was available for them. The young men in their age-villages were able to obtain sufficient arable land and they were able to establish their economic independence after marriage, if not earlier. Because land was plentiful there was little real concern for security of tenure and disputes over land were both uncommon and unimportant.

By 1955 the basic fact was that there was insufficient land to meet the people's requirements in the alluvial flood plains – as also in many Highland areas – and there remained little or no unused land which could be taken into cultivation.

Inheritance of Land

In those earlier and more spacious days, inheritance was chiefly signifi-cant in moveable property – cattle pre-eminently, and goats, money and other goods – and also in the matter of widows and the custody of children. The rules of inheritance were the same in principle for all this property. Inheritance was by groups of full-brothers rather than by individuals, and therefore when a man died, his sons, his widows and his wealth were taken by the eldest surviving full-brother; failing a full-brother, a half-brother would inherit (the eldest surviving at the time). Only when all the deceased's brothers were dead, or if they had moved away and severed practical relations, were the dead man's sons able to take up the property in their own right. Then each group of full-brothers tended to inherit as separate, corporate groups. Although the separation into "houses" was not as strong and notable as amongst some African peoples,[1] yet there was a fairly strong solidarity between full-brothers such that, for instance, their cattle were regarded as a distinct and separate herd, over which the senior brother had principal control and in which half-brothers had little direct rights.

Originally land inheritance did not follow this scheme because it was an unimportant matter, for ideally a man obtained his building plot and arable land at the time of the formal establishment of his age-village, and he preferred if possible to continue to live amongst his coevals. Consequently, when a man died, his brothers and his sons and nephews normally had land of their own and did not wish for more elsewhere, especially as the deceased's land would probably be in another age-village. Out of respect for the dead man and his contemporaries, the chief heir often made a token residence at the deceased's homestead and then, after a brief period, would obtain the approval of the villagers to return to his own village and holding again – perhaps at the cost of some beer or a goat. Sometimes the heir or another member of the lineage might take the opportunity to leave his own village

---

1. See Wilson, M. 1950, pp. 117ff. Cf. also my *The Family Herds*, London, 1955, Chapters 3 and 4, for a description of a strong, corporate 'house' system.

(e.g. for fear of witchcraft) and take up the vacant holding. Nevertheless in general the holding was allowed to lapse and it could be re-allocated by the village headman if need arose; or the elderly widows might be allowed to continue to reside and cultivate as long as they wished.

Once land began to become scarce and valuable this loose system could no longer continue. Junior brothers and half-brothers were no longer content to permit the chief heir to take the whole of the deceased's holding to do with it as he wished, and a systematised division had to be adopted. At first, naturally enough, land was gradually brought under the same system which controlled the inheritance of other property, but this proved inadequate – inadequate not only in itself as being, perhaps, too complicated and conducive of disagreement and quarrelling in so far as land is concerned, but also because that system itself was already beginning to break down under the impact of individualism.

It was felt that because sons assist their father in his homestead and fields and in their turn rely on him for a share in the cash-and-kind profits of peasant farming, therefore they should have priority in the inheritance of their father's property. Their father's brothers, it was said, would in any case already have their own holdings in which likewise their sons have prime interest. Conversely, older Nyakyusa men began to be reluctant to take a brother's land (and other property too) on his death, for fear that, in their turn, control of their own land would descend at their deaths to their brothers' sons rather than to their own sons.

As a result of these attitudes a strong desire arose to modify the customary laws in this matter, and the Rungwe African District Council, with the approval of the Government, has by formal resolution established a new law under which sons may inherit direct from their own fathers.

This law is not universally accepted by the Nyakyusa of the Lake Plains and sons still will sometimes waive their novel rights in favour of the traditional claims of their fathers' brothers. They say that they do not desire to see the break up of the wider lineage which, in effect, this new law encourages; they are also afraid of the anger and jealousy, and thus of the witchcraft, of their uncles. It appears however that the change is accepted by the large majority of the people, for it follows the trend of modern values and kinship sentiments.

The principal heir is now the eldest son, but in general he has little direct control over the property and land of his half-brothers unless they are still young, in which case he has a moral duty to act as guardian and custodian. Sons inherit that part of the paternal holding which had been allocated to their mother by their father in his lifetime, plus any other pieces he might have given to any of them direct as individuals. Each group of full-brothers determines the way in which it divides up its own inheritance. The eldest brother of such a house has a definite obligation to see that his juniors obtain shares of the land in so far as its extent and their number will allow. On the whole it is expected by Nyakyusa that the eldest brother will secure the best holding for himself, as befits his new status, but he cannot deny his younger brothers' claims. Disputes in this matter are not uncommon and the local courts have already shown their determination to support the claims of younger brothers.

Very commonly – though it has not yet crystallised as compulsory social behaviour – a father will grant a portion of his holding to his son on the latter's marriage, or as soon after as the son decides to give up labour migration and settle down. It is thought that a married man should be independent economically and that he should be able to maintain his own household; it is realised that there is most likely to be friction in the relations between father and son, especially in this society where it is traditionally

21

believed that parents and children should live apart.[1] In the same way, and for similar reasons, an elder brother tries to make provision for his junior when the latter marries if their father is already dead. The practice of the father is not a legally required one, although it is nowadays increasingly common and sons have begun to expect it: the practice of an elder brother is now legally required in the matter of land and probably always has been in the matter of cattle.

The difficulties are obvious when a man dies and leaves several sons but only a small-sized holding. To date no clear ruling has emerged and unfortunately the African District Council did not deal specifically with such details when introducing the new law. How much land an eldest brother can reasonably retain for himself is perhaps not determinable in practice except in specific relation to the nature, locality and fertility of the holding in question, the plots already held by the man himself, the needs and number of the younger brothers and any holdings they may have, and the location of the villages in which they severally live. There is also plenty of scope for disagreement between half-brothers over portions of the paternal holding which had been retained by the father himself for his own use; over portions allocated to a wife who has borne no sons or whose sons have died, and over permanent trees. The situation is still fluid and there has not yet been time enough for a common and generally acceptable solution to be established. Consequently each group of sons tries to solve its own particular problems in this matter as best it can, torn between old values and new attitudes and needs.

Relations between both full-brothers and half-brothers tend often to be severely tried at times of inheritance. It is not primarily, I think, a case of brothers' greed for valued land tending to overcome bonds of fraternity and co-operation; but it is rather that a father's arable holding is often not able to provide adequate amounts of arable land for each of his sons, and yet they find the very greatest difficulty in obtaining land elsewhere. Already the traditional kin-group comprising the sons and grandsons of a group of full-brothers had begun to break down even before land shortage became serious. Now the group of full-brothers itself tends to be dispersed as men obtain land where they can and it is endangered by dissensions over land rights and land division. Increasingly, it seems, a Nyakyusa man is becoming detached from his brothers and he tends to establish an independent family unit comprising his immediate family alone – that is, himself with his wives and children. We cannot attribute the whole cause of this modern trend to land shortage and economic difficulties, of course, for involved also are new ideas of individualism and of personal effort and reward, and the decreasing need for the consistent support of brothers in social, economic and ritual activities.

Younger brothers may, and sometimes do in fact, agree that the paternal holding is already too small for further sub-division, or that the small parts which can be made available to them are scarcely worth having – especially if they live some distance away. On the other hand, the eldest brother may already have obtained a holding in his own village and is therefore willing to make only a small claim or none at all in the interests of his juniors, and he may then divide the inheritance amongst them alone. Usually, so acute is the dearth of land, the holding is divided between two or more brothers. It is split into small plots so that each brother has a share of paddy, food-crop and banana land, and these are commonly a half acre or even less in size nowadays. As already mentioned, by a kind of modern equity the local African courts generally favour the claims of the younger

---

1. See Wilson, M., 1951, p. 159 and *passim*. "The overt purpose (of age-villages) is the separation of sons and mothers, of fathers-in-law and daughters-in-law." (*Ibid* p. 162).

brothers, and this is compelling the increasing and continued fragmentation of holdings at time of inheritance. Even so, if there are several brothers (i.e., sons of the deceased) the youngest among them may still be unable to obtain a plot, or at least not one of an economically viable size, and they are then compelled to try to gain admittance to some other village as newcomers, there to be allocated land.

The shortage of land is, therefore, not only making inheritance very considerably more important, but it is assisting in the establishment of new kinship attitudes and a redefining of fraternal relations. The position is most confused at the moment as the old system continues to exist alongside the new, sometimes more or less successfully, but often in intractable opposition. At the present time the observer can only mention general tendencies, for it is impossible as yet to foresee what the eventual result will be, and there are, in any case, many other factors involved besides those of the inheritance of scarce land.

In so far as we are primarily concerned with land problems in this essay, the basic factors are that land is newly scarce, that there is virtually no alternative activity in the country to the arable use of the land, and that therefore each son must try to obtain a share in the often inadequate holding of his father. I suggest that no form of inheritance can deal with such a situation satisfactorily – at least it is highly doubtful if any has yet emerged in an area of land shortage in Eastern Africa – and thus there are bound to be severe difficulties and a deterioration of inter-personal relations between near kinsmen who are most in competition. The new inheritance law of the Nyakyusa has narrowed the range of potential conflict from the patrilineal descendants of a grandfather to the sons of a single father; but if it has obviated possible hostility between the generations and between paternal cousins, it has also removed much of the common interest and mutual inter-dependence between them.

The Right to Land, and the Authority of the Village Headman

Although the traditional principle still exists that every villager has a right to arable land within the village boundaries, yet it is no longer possible to carry it out in practice. Every village headman, in my experience, attempts to ensure that each of his men has land, but he cannot always succeed, and most especially he cannot provide every one with as much land as he would like, because of sheer spatial limitation.

Nowhere any longer does the old principle now hold that an established villager may, without permission or notification, take vacant land into cultivation as part of his holding. When land becomes vacant it must now revert immediately to the village as a group, that is to the common pool from which the headman as village authority makes allocations. There are so many and such varied demands for land nowadays that no man acting on his own can presume to take up vacant land, and only the headman may decide allocation. No person can now obtain land, whether he be an established villager or not, unless he is allocated it by the headman – or, in the many large villages typical of the Lake Plains, by the headman's assistant, *ugwakyimo*, who is delegated authority in a section of the village.

Land becomes vacant when a man shifts to another village, when a man dies and leaves no active heir who desires to take up the deceased's holding, or (but seldom today) when a man gives up part of his holding due to his inability to use the whole of it. In all these cases the land is immediately re-allocated by the headman, probably not as a single unit any longer, as best he can among a crowd of land-hungry villagers – established men seeking extra land to meet the needs of growing families or for increasing cash-crop

23

production, young men seeking their own independent holding, and new-comers to the villages who seek to settle there.

The modern shortage of land has therefore considerably increased the authority and the activities of the village headman. Nowadays he is the prime mover in all changes in land-holding, other than by inheritance or temporary loans and gifts. In these latter, and particularly in inheritance, he has necessarily become an important interested party whose influence cannot be ignored, whose approval is desired and whose assistance is fre-quently sought both as arbiter and witness. Much more than before, and directly because of the scarcity and value of land today, he is the principal controller and allocator of land – though, of course, he remains subject to the state of public feeling and the opinions of his villagers. His position has been further strengthened by his status at the base of the administrative hierarchy in modern local government, whereby he is given executive responsibility for his village and its people. As always, disputes over land are taken before him in the first instance and here he acts not only as a judge but also as the expositor of village opinion and public knowledge. Such disputes are increasing in number, giving him more work and re-sponsibility and also more opportunity for the expression of his status. Meanwhile his traditionally crucial ritual and magical (anti-witchcraft) powers continue, though now in somewhat attentuated form.

Fragmentation and Dispersion of Holdings

It has been shown how the inheritance of land, now of increasing importance, results normally in the splitting up of a man's holding.[1] Whether a young man obtains an inherited share of his father's land or he obtains an allocation in another village, its size is likely to be small – smaller than the holdings of his father's generation. Tiny, uneconomic plots are to be seen everywhere in the flood plains.

At the same time a man's holding is tending to comprise a scattered, heterogeneous collection of small plots, as he has obtained land when and where he could. An actual example will illustrate this: a young man had about a tenth of an acre behind his house on which he was growing maize and beans; he had about a quarter of an acre which was his share of his deceased father's land, and another quarter of an acre which had been allocated to him by the headman when a vacated holding was split up, and on both of these he cultivated paddy. This man had only small hope of obtaining more land, unless one of his brothers died without sons, for he had already been refused by the headman a share in a recently vacated holding on the grounds that, unlike many of his contemporaries, he already had at least some arable land.

Even amongst older men the holding of scattered plots is common. This is partly the result of the earlier expansion of cultivation when the formerly unused lands were put under paddy, and partly because older men too, lose no opportunity, in the face of scarcity, to take up any land they can. The Nyakyusa ideal is to have a single large holding, preferably stretching away behind the homestead – or alternatively two fields, one for paddy out in the open plains and one for food crops nearer home. This ideal becomes less and less practicable. There seems to be little or no need for this scatter of plots on account of soil and fertility differences, for these are generally few and unimportant within the area of a single village.

In my sample villages the average number of separate plots was about three per holding. There was a notable difference between villages in relation to the average size of villagers' holdings. Where land was more plentiful the

---

1. If there is only one son to inherit the holding, it is most likely that he will have to give way to the pressing demands of his father's brothers' sons if he is not to cut himself off from his lineage.

24

number of separate plots per holding was less than where land was scarcer; at the same time the average size of separate plots was smaller in those more land-hungry villages. The reader may refer to Table III (page 15) for some illustrative figures. Though differences are not yet very great, nevertheless there seems to be a fairly clear correlation between the average size of villagers' holdings on the one hand, and on the other the number and size of separate plots, and this is entirely borne out by my general information obtained in villages where actual measurements were not made. The inescapable conclusion must be that increasing scarcity of land in the Lake Plains leads to increasing fragmentation and dispersion of holdings; further, the present land situation and land tenure system can only lead to a continuation of this trend.

To emphasise the actual situation in 1955, let me reiterate the results of my own village surveys in the very high density region. In a village in Koroso's chiefdom only a quarter of the younger men had paddy land of their own, holdings averaging about three-quarters of an acre; in a village in Mwakipesile's chiefdom, only 17 per cent. of the younger men had paddy land and holdings averaged about half an acre (cf. Table VII, page 37). These two examples are taken from the areas of most severe land shortage and are not therefore altogether typical of the whole Lake Plains. Nevertheless, I do not think that they are entirely atypical; more importantly, they indicate the present trend. Within another generation this fragmentation and scatter of holdings may well be the common feature everywhere in the flood plains unless the system of tenure and inheritance is modified. If the increase in population is quickened through improved medical facilities, better diet and housing, and improved conditions generally, then the position will become more acute. Such an increase is only to be expected. The Nyakyusa have decisively entered a money economy and they have learnt to seek higher standards of living. Only from their fields, by cash-cropping, can they expect to earn their livings and the demand for better living will not be curtailed – nor, of course, is it desirable that it should be.

There is another aspect of this whole matter which must be considered. It relates to the movement of individuals between villages. Such movement was, in earlier European days, a crucial factor in the age-village structure, for it was not only exceedingly frequent, but also it tended to undermine the idealised coeval basis of village life. Movement between villages is increasingly difficult now, for a newcomer naturally cannot easily obtain land, nor as much land as he would desire even at a moderate demand. Nevertheless, the reasons for movement persist, and they will do so whilst the fear of witchcraft remains and whilst illness and misfortune are attributable to the unfavourable aura of a place. There remains also the tradition of moving so that a man may escape from bad relations with kinsfolk or neighbours, or from the obloquy resulting from his own disapproved actions. Much social and psychological tension is being created now as a result of the new difficulty of movement, and so far the Nyakyusa have not evolved alternative methods.

On the other hand, so deeply engrained is the notion of the prestige and power which accrues to a village by virtue of the number of its inhabitants, that headmen and villagers alike remain most reluctant to refuse to accept newcomers, even when it inevitably means that the present inhabitants must meet a further decrease in the average amount of land available per family, for a newcomer must be allocated a holding if he is to remain. Consequently, if a holding is for any reason left vacant, a headman tends to refuse to re-allocate some or all of it amongst his villagers and thus to augment their holdings; but instead he keeps it in reserve pending the hoped-for arrival of another newcomer. Men desiring to leave their own village try to get

C

news of such reserved land elsewhere. Such land is cultivated in the meantime on a kind of year-to-year lease by one or more of the villagers as allowed by the headman.

Even when no vacant plots exist a headman will still accept newcomers. If they are young men they must be prepared to go landless for the time being (i.e., to remain dependent on their father's fields elsewhere) until such time as land becomes vacant. If the newcomer is an older man, then the headman will try to persuade one or more of his villagers to give up portions of their holdings and he will often cede part of his own land. The newcomer is therefore often allocated small strips and plots here and there in the village arable area and he thereafter joins the land-hungry crowd seeking to expand their holdings. In one village in which I worked where land shortage was critical (Kapugi, Koroso's chiefdom), there was not a single patch of usable land unworked; yet here the headman had, with full village approval, accepted three newcomers during the first nine months of 1955. Two of them were young men, one unmarried, and they could not expect to obtain land for some time except for a small banana plot. The third newcomer was a middle-aged man from a village some 12 miles away in another chiefdom. The headman had given him a half-acre plot out of his own paddy field and was laboriously begging pieces of land here and there from his people in order to make up a new holding of perhaps an acre. The headman himself had only about three and a half acres of arable land; he had at least one adult son who had not yet acquired an arable plot and he had other sons and brothers' sons owning only small fields. Yet he favoured this stranger, this newcomer. He was quite firm in his resolution to accept other newcomers in the future and in this he believed that he was acting as a good headman should. As far as I could learn he was supported by his villagers.

This is not, by any means, an isolated or even unusual phenomenon. It is, I feel, important to bear in mind this illustration of contemporary affairs. Firstly, because it shows another way in which holdings are fragmented and dispersed; and secondly, because it demonstrates how, so far, the Nyakyusa have refused to face the situation of land shortage, and how they continue to follow traditional practices and values associated with village prestige. These people complain of their inability to obtain sufficient arable land, but they are not yet prepared to make the mental and social adjustments which might at least partly relieve their new predicament. On the other hand, they themselves understand the need for movement and perhaps they are right in their implied insistence not to discard their cultural ideals. Their insistence on accepting newcomers and their willingness (however dimly perceived and expressed) to share their land with the landless are not discreditable attitudes, even if they are economically untenable.

Security of Tenure and Disputes over Land

As already noted, under traditional land tenure a Nyakyusa had good security in his holding so long as he continued to live in the same village. The only alteration of tenure occurred at the "coming-out" ceremony of a new chief when the older men would, if required, move aside in order to give their sons' generation the best land. This did not invariably happen in any case. Fundamentally, however, security of tenure is not a matter of great importance to a people who have plenty of land, and land which is more or less of the same quality. Indeed, convenience of location in respect of one's own homestead was almost the only value land had as such. Occasionally a more dominant chief might try to seize a commoner's field to allow of his own expanded cultivation; it was most unusual for him to succeed, and even if he did the dispossessed villager suffered little real deprivation, for he could easily obtain another field fairly near at hand.

26

Security of tenure has continued into European times, and although perhaps weakened slightly in one way through the exaggerated powers which accrue to modern Government-supported chiefs, it has been strengthened by the modern peace and rule of law and the more efficient system of justice provided by the established local courts. According to G. Wilson (Wilson, G., 1938, p. 32) the increase in the movement of individuals between villages in earlier European times (i.e., up to about 1940-45) directly caused a lack of attachment to individual plots, and thus security of tenure was not considered particularly important.

The new situation of land shortage does not affect the basic position, or rather, by producing a high scarcity value on land, it has brought about an intensification of individuals' rights over their holdings. No longer dare a chief or headman attempt to commit such illegal acts as the seizure of a villager's field, so long as that villager is not afraid to publicise the affair. A man is not, and cannot afford to be, prepared to lose his field, for he cannot replace it with any certainty, either in a convenient location or elsewhere. A headman may sometimes bring strong pressure to bear on some of the men of his village to try to persuade them to give up portions of their land to assist a newcomer or a landless neighbour, but a villager can and does refuse and there is no legal authority which can override him here. As the land shortage becomes more obvious and more acute so men become less willing to allow their holdings to be touched for any reason, by anyone. The re-allocation at a "coming-out" ceremony appears to have been dropped nowadays[1] and thus a man holds his land undisturbed until his death, when it passes by inheritance to his sons. There are cases now where grandsons of the original holder occupy land through undisturbed and undisputed inheritance. A man can, as he wishes, loan a kinsman or friend a plot in his holding, or he can make an outright gift. The principal restriction which remains is that a man must continue to live in the village in order to retain these rights; he must relinquish them if he permanently goes to live elsewhere. Nevertheless, the land of a well-established villager would be kept for him pending his hoped-for return, for if he has left in umbrage and fear because of suspected witchcraft, then he may be persuaded to come back after a time. The headman and his neighbours should in fact persist in their attempts to persuade him, even to the use of force, for this is not only a moral duty of age-mates and fellow-villagers but is also an effort to remove the implications of their alleged witchcraft and anti-social conduct.

Once, therefore, a man obtains land he has absolute rights in it during his continued residence in the village. Especially today, older men seldom shift their homes and almost all land is now held on a tenure which will be passed on by inheritance.

Boundary disputes are few. Usually, and increasingly, village boundaries are well known, and field boundaries invariably are. During my field measurements in the sample villages, I never met any difficulty with my local teams in quickly establishing the ownership and exact limits of any plot. Boundaries are usually marked by small ridges of accumulated debris or by narrow paths, and these form an intricate and irregular network throughout a village's arable area. They are so well known that there is very little scope for a greedy man to attempt to encroach on a neighbour's holding at hoeing time. If minor disagreements do arise at that season they can be immediately settled – by appeal to neighbours working nearby if necessary – and the headman or his assistant may well not be called in at

---

1. This is the case in the Lake Plains. In some of the more conservative Highland chiefdoms where the cash economy is less advanced and land scarcity is not serious, there still appears to be some re-allocation in favour of the young men in the traditional way. In general, however, it is clear that the traditional age-village system of land allocation is obsolete; see pages 29ff.

all. Field boundaries have lost their earlier fluidity, when a plenty of land did not call for precise demarcation, and the only important changes now result from the land being left vacant or by the internal division of established holdings by inheritance or anticipatory inheritance.

In brief, then, the high premium given to land because of its modern scarcity value, and the enhanced authority of the headman in land affairs act together to preserve the individual's rights. The residual rights of the village, as group-owner of all land within the village boundary, do not affect the land-holder during his continued residence there.

The commonest type of dispute in land matters arises in inheritance, where a younger brother sues his senior in order to obtain or increase his share of the paternal holding (see page 21). That is to say, in general only where established holdings are being broken up does dispute arise and then, of course, only between the sons of the dead man. Disputes between neighbours in a village seldom are grave enough to be brought to court or even before the headman.

There are also many petty, semi-domestic cases which faithfully reflect the frequently poor relations between Nyakyusa husbands and wives in modern times.[1]

TABLE IV
NYAKYUSA LAND DISPUTES: CIVIL CASES, 1954

	No. of civil cases	Land cases No.	%	Population per land case	Density of population
Lake Plains	1,977	104	5	567	285
N.E. Highlands	965	24	2.5	1,842	199
Central Region	901	13	1.5	4,092	245
N.W. Highlands	1,280	8	0.6	7,300	201

Based on returns of civil cases in local courts of first instance ('B' Courts) for 1954. In 1955 the percentages were almost exactly the same as in 1954.

Several interesting points are suggested by these figures. Firstly, there is the larger proportion of land cases and the much smaller population per case in the Lake Plains, where land shortage is worst in relation to local demand, not only because of the higher density of population as such, but also because of the relatively larger acreages required for paddy cultivation. Secondly, in the Central Region of Nyakyusa country there is also a high density of population, but nevertheless only a few land cases; this may be attributed to the absence of cash-cropping and the absence, therefore, of a keen demand for land. On the other hand, the relatively numerous cases, or small population per case, in the north-eastern Highlands seem to result directly from a particularly densely populated area (Mwakaleli) where coffee cultivation is long established and the demand for land is exceptionally keen. In other words, as far as the figures for 1954 and 1955 show, there is a direct connection between land scarcity and the incidence of land disputes before the local courts (i.e. the more intractable disputes which go beyond the village headmen). General observation supports this conclusion. It may be expected in the future, therefore, that such cases will increase unless administrative action is taken to rationalise the inheritance laws with a view to minimising the area of potential disagreement amongst the sons of a deceased man.

For comparative interest, in so far as they offer some indication, I append here data on other Districts in the Territory where land disputes are common.

---

1. In 1954, 68 per cent. of all civil cases in the lowest courts were marital disputes, including divorce suits, and there was one divorce case for every 24 adult males living in the country in that year.

SKETCH PLAN OF KAPUGI VILLAGE, KOROSO'S CHIEFDOM, 1955.

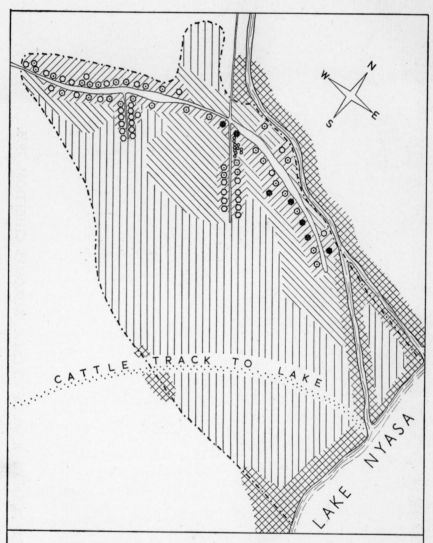

SKETCH PLAN OF KAPUGI VILLAGE, KOROSO'S CHIEFDOM, 1955

-REFERENCE-

HUT OR HOMESTEAD OF:

● MAN OVER 55 YEARS

◉ MAN ABOUT 30-55 YEARS

○ MAN ABOUT 17-30 YEARS

∘ YOUTH OR BOY

—·—·— VILLAGE BOUNDARY

▨ BANANAS AND OTHER TREES (CITRUS, MANGO, FIREWOOD, ETC)

▨ MAIZE AND BEANS

▥ PADDY (THE PARTS NEARER THE HOMESTEADS ARE USED IN THE DRY SEASON FOR BEANS, MAIZE)

▨ SEDGE AND REED THICKET

TABLE V
DISTRICTS IN TANGANYIKA WHERE LAND DISPUTES ARE COMMON

1953	No. of land cases	% of total civil cases	Estimated population density	Population per land case
Bukoba District	1,189	23	69	223
Lushoto Division	149	12	188	742
Moshi District	347	25	277	746
Ngara District	81	29	125	1,393

The Changing Village

The possibly unique age-village of the Nyakyusa is now undergoing considerable and fairly rapid change in response to the new conditions of land shortage. There is, firstly, an increasing sense of village exclusiveness and, secondly, there has been a breakdown in the essential age-basis of its organisation. That is to say, that whilst the corporate unity of the village as an independent group has been strengthened, yet the social foundation of the village has simultaneously been changed and a different sort of village is emerging. It would take us far beyond the scope of this present essay if a full analysis of the changing village were to be made, nevertheless in so far as these changes are more or less directly the consequences of modern land shortage, land tenure and economic conditions some account is essential. Since the age-village was fundamental in the life and social organisation of these people, the new emerging village is of crucial importance.

Land shortage has definitely exaggerated the unity and exclusiveness of the village in the Lake Plains at a time when, for other reasons, it was beginning to become a more open group. There was always, as we have seen, insistence on the principle that only a member of the village could hold and use village land; but village boundaries were often poorly marked and it was difficult to determine which headman, if any, had genuine jurisdiction over land relatively distant from the established village sites. Nor was it particularly important to be able to do so whilst land was plentiful. As paddy cultivation spread, men began seeking extra fields farther and farther away from home as land nearby was all taken up; and so long as they did not attempt to take land in the immediate vicinity of another village site there was seldom much difficulty in this. The attitudes born of a sufficiency of land persisted and headmen were not disposed to protest against outsiders who sought fields near the limits of their vaguely defined areas. Internecine warfare and raiding had, of course, been abolished as an expression of and a weapon in inter-village rivalries and animosities. With the establishment of general peace and security, and with increasing movement about the country between villages and chiefdoms, such rivalries and animosities began to die away. Many men came to live in the villages which they themselves had not helped to found; their coevals from their fathers' villages lived elsewhere, many of them widely scattered, and it was not possible to maintain a high degree of village patriotism, and, people began to feel, it was not especially necessary or important any longer.

It began to be possible for a man to hold some of his arable land within the area of another village, so long as members of the second village were not deprived of the opportunity of their own agricultural expansion should they desire it. This was especially the case when a large area of hitherto vacant (i.e. bush) but now valuable paddy land was contained within the approximate boundaries of a village. Outsiders were allowed to acquire fields on the strength of kinship with the headman or with one of the established villagers, or even by giving some small present to the headman (e.g. a little beer or some meat, etc.). Land was still plentiful then, or so it seemed to the Nyakyusa, and future shortages and difficulties were not perceived.

Thus beyond the established fields in the vicinity of the village itself, the pattern of land holding tended to become confused. The majority of land-holders were still members of the village who were expanding their cultivation outwards, but there was a considerable number of men from neighbouring villages, and even from farther afield where opportunities were more restricted. Some men even began to have a second house, inhabitated by a junior wife, in another village from which to continue the more easily the cultivation of new holdings.

This sort of development was in the event only a short-term process and, had pressure of population on the land not become so critical, it is not possible to say what would have been the final result upon Nyakyusa social and village organisation. It is, nevertheless, important to note that in the beginnings of the extension of arable holdings, cash-crop cultivation operated in a system in which village exclusiveness was breaking down, when residence was no longer an essential prerequisite of land-holding, and when men were neighbours in the fields as farmers without being coevals of a single village.

Once the Nyakyusa, and particularly the more perceptive headmen, began to realise that land was becoming less plentiful, indeed that it was beginning to be scarce in relation to new demands, this novel tendency was stopped fairly quickly and the old traditional principle of land-holding only by residence was reasserted. In the most recent years this has been strongly insisted on. Headmen and their villagers saw that in order to safeguard their own rights they must prevent scarce, valuable land being held and used by outsiders. This reaction appears to have been universal and automatic among the Nyakyusa. There was now insufficient land for everyone's demands and each village therefore looked after what it considered to be its own interests. Outsiders who already held fields could not be deprived of them, but they were not allowed to extend their holdings and every opportunity was, and still is, taken to regain control of their fields for allocation to villagers proper. Inheritance was often disallowed unless the heir agreed to come and live permanently in the village; gifts or loans to outsiders (kin or friends) were no longer permitted and most headmen seized the opportunity to re-allocate to their own villagers any alien-held plots which were not consistently maintained in cultivation.

In response to the new situation, almost everywhere village boundaries were clearly demarcated – not without a certain amount of dispute and a new recognition of inter-village opposition. Nowhere now is it possible for a man to take up land over which there is no firmly established village ownership. The significant principle has now emerged that not only does a village, as a corporate and distinct group, own its own land and is represented in this by its headman; but all land is now owned by some village. Further, at least in the high-density regions, there is no longer any vacant land to be taken up and any land temporarily falling vacant comes immediately under the allocating authority of the headman.

This process, the application of this principle, is not yet quite universal in the Lake Plains, and it is sometimes still possible to see it coming into operation. Still in the northerly parts of the Lake Plains – the low-density region – one may see fields occupied by a variety of outsiders, for there the realisation of the significance of land shortage has been slowest to come. For example, in Mwakipesile's chiefdom in the late 1940s and early 1950s it was the practice of men from the congested villages nearer the Lake to obtain valuable, virgin paddy land in the newly opened areas in the north (near Ipinda) without residential qualifications. Many men reserved their original holdings in their own villages for food crops and had their main paddy fields in this distant area. By 1955, however, it had become virtually impossible for a non-resident to obtain extra land in this way, although still there remained scattered pieces here and there which could be taken up, and some existing holdings in the area are too large for the agricultural capabilities of their occupiers. The temporary safety valve was shut off. The local headman had become seriously worried over the large-scale alienation of his land resources without any equivalent increase in the number of his villagers, and he also wished to conserve the remaining land against the now better understood needs of his own people.

The principle of no land without residence also means that a villager who wishes to move must automatically forfeit his land-holding in the village. A little earlier he would most probably have been able to retain at least his fields beyond the immediate vicinity of the houses – in so far as his new residence was not too far away to allow continued cultivation. This has been especially important for younger men who, wishing to take up a vacant holding elsewhere, also desire to retain their share of the paternal holding obtained by inheritance. Conversely, they are now unable to move on to their father's holding and yet retain their fields in their own village. Such men must now make a permanent decision between the utility of, perhaps, two inadequate holdings which, however, combined together might be of satisfactory size.

As a consequence of this, inter-village opposition is probably greater than it has ever been in European times, and no less strong perhaps than it was in the old days. Men feel that the security of their holdings, the future of their sons, and the possibility of increasing their arable cultivation lies wholly within the security and stability of their own village. They tend to see other villages and other villagers as a potential threat to their own land requirements; they often suspect the worst of neighbouring villages who, they think, will, given the chance, seize some of their land. Headmen and villagers would refuse to cross the boundary into another village when they accompanied me during my investigations, lest they be accused of contemplating appropriation of the land there. Such aliens who still retained land in a village were regarded with some animosity. Nyakyusa would not look beyond their own village boundaries in an attempt to make an appreciation of the modern overall land situation. They wished only tenaciously to cling to what they already had and to guard it jealously; they were only too inclined to believe that other villages nearby were better off and to use them as scapegoats for their own difficulties and shortage. It must be said that this renewed insistence on village exclusiveness and the inviolability of village boundaries has in fact tended to make for a certain inequality of land-holding according to the perceptiveness and celerity with which headmen claimed authority over formerly vacant lands. This condition is, however, overexaggerated in men's claims today, and in any case it is tending to disappear under the pressure of inter-village movement.

The Nyakyusa village in the Lake Plains, with its intensified independence and aggressive exclusiveness, and jealous of its believed permanent boundaries, has not at the same time been able to retain its traditional coeval basis. Whereas formerly the youths of a village moved to one side, there to build their own hamlet and eventually to acquire their own fields in association with its establishment as a full village in its own right, now this is no longer feasible or even possible, for the land is not available for this sort of expansion. The young men are driven back on a dependence on the fields already held by their fathers in the old village. They gradually move into their fathers' places and take over the paternal holdings; or, as we have seen, they seek where they may to obtain new allocations in any other village where they can gain admittance. The coeval basis of village living is lost.

The boys and youths still leave their fathers' houses and build their first, small huts together on a site somewhere adjacent to the main village site, as determined by the village headman. But even building sites with the essentially associated banana groves are becoming increasingly scarce and valuable, for no one desires to decrease the amount of arable by enlarging the built-up areas – rather the reverse. The number of young men's villages is therefore diminishing and congestion of their huts is increasing to the stage very often where no more than a narrow passage if left between adjacent houses. There comes to be a wider age range in the young men's hamlets where, often, a large village provides only one for all its sons. Smaller villages sometimes provide no accommodation at all for their sons, who are thus compelled to seek membership of a neighbouring group. These hamlets are mainly regarded nowadays as temporary residential areas for the young men until such time as they move on to an existing holding – their father's or some other. There is therefore no attempt to provide sufficient space for an adequate banana grove with each young man's house, let alone a food-crop plot behind it. The arable land beyond the congested huts already belongs to inhabitants of the main village. When a young man is able to leave and take up a holding, his vacated site (together, often, with the hut) is taken over by a waiting youth who has probably been sharing with another hitherto.

These young men's hamlets do not, any longer, eventually mature and become villages in their own right with their own headman and arable lands. Formerly, when this occurred, they would probably have taken over a good deal of the lands of the old village, as the young men exercised the privileges of their new maturity against their elders with the emergence of the new chiefdom. New chiefdoms, and with them new villages, no longer emerge, and this is mainly because Government has prohibited the bifurcation of petty chiefdoms on the death of the old chief, as it is considered inconsistent with the development of stable, modern local government. Additionally, however, the shortage of land can no longer allow of the traditional expanding politico-territorial organisation. The elder men's villages are not now prepared to yield ground to the young men, and the latter cannot expand elsewhere. Thus political requirements and land restriction work together to make the old system obsolete and to freeze the spatial distribution of villages as it existed in early European times. As far as I could ascertain in the chiefdoms of the Lake Plains, probably no new village had emerged in the past 20 or more years, except for a few cases of large ones splitting into two for administrative and social convenience. Many villages there date back to pre-European days often now under the son, or even the grandson, of the original headman (though this is not essential or invariable in any way).

The age-basis of the Nyakyusa village is thus disappearing; indeed, in many villages it has already disappeared in everything but the young men's hamlets. Where the process has gone least far, there is still apparent a rough division of the single village into the old men's sector (men at least 50 years of age, and many much older); the middle-aged men's sector (men between about 30 and 50 years old, being the younger brothers or elder sons of the old men); and the young men's and youths' sector. On inheritance, sons tend to show a continued reluctance to move and live on their father's house-site and to become immediate neighbours of older men; they avoid it if possible, often allowing a middle-aged man to shift there instead. Nevertheless even this sort of age-division is rapidly vanishing and in very many villages a man's neighbour may be of any age.

We have seen that inheritance is now one of the chief methods of obtaining land. Under the new inheritance rules, this means that sons follow their fathers and take up their fathers' arable holdings, building sites and banana groves. Some young men inherit early, others inherit late; there is no longer any notion or possibility of the younger generation entering into its

32

land en bloc. Young men compete with one another, with their elder brothers and with their fathers for allocations of land left vacant. We also saw, however, that often in the larger families[1] not all the sons are able to get a share of the paternal holding, or at least not a share of practicable size. Thus younger sons are forced to resort to trying to obtain vacant land elsewhere – possibly within the same village, but as often as not outside. Finally, the young man on his new holding may find his neighbours to be of any age; certainly they will not have been members of his own original coeval hamlet.

The way for this changing concept of village life and the new sort of village was prepared in the years before land shortage became important. The changed political system has been briefly noted already, but no less important was the great increase in inter-village movement in earlier European days when peace and personal security had been established. During this period Wilson (1938, page 32) reckoned that perhaps 80 per cent. of Nyakyusa shifted at least once from the place where they first obtained fields. This estimate, whilst perhaps holding good for Highland Nyakyusa amongst whom Wilson mainly worked, was too high for the people of the Lake Plains, where about 40 per cent. is more correct according to my genealogical and village surveys. That is still a relatively high degree of mobility for a mainly subsistence, peasant society such as it was in those years. It is clear that the pseudo-fraternal bond of coevality could not persist as a main element of village life and consciousness, when in fact as many as half of the members of a village were not original coeval founders but had come in from elsewhere. Before the land shortage, movement did not entail the shifting of young men to other young men's villages, or of older men to other older men's villages. It was, at least eventually, promiscuous movement, ignoring age categories. The compulsions of land shortage seem, in retrospect, only to have followed existing lines of village development and to have begun the completion of the process.

In the Lake Plains, therefore, the village persists as a close, territorial, land-owning group and as a specific cluster of homesteads and huts, usually with a village street, the whole closely hemmed in by continuous banana groves. Beyond this lie the arable lands, usually food-crop fields nearby and paddy fields farther off. In jealously protecting what it already holds, the village has gained a new exclusiveness, for the security of the individual land-holder is maintained by the corporate ownership of the village and by excluding outsiders as far as possible. On the other hand, it is no longer an age-village either in fact or intention, and it cannot be, for age-villages were consistent only with an expanding territorial system and a subsistence economy.

This brief analysis of Nyakyusa village organisation in recent times applies only to the Lake Plains. In some parts of both the Central Region and the Northern Highlands the age-basis of Nyakyusa villages had most probably already been seriously weakened in pre-European times.[2] On the other hand, elsewhere, and particularly in the more conservative parts less affected by modern trends and the cash economy, the traditional age-village still exists in something like its old form.

Land shortage has appeared in the Highlands together with a developing cash economy, but the basis of agricultural and economic change lies mainly in coffee cultivation which, of course, requires relatively smaller fields than does paddy in the Lake Plains, but it needs more care and attention from the grower for moderate success. As far as I could see in the course of

---

1. Polygny is still the norm amongst the older and many middle-aged men, and therefore a father often leaves several sons to inherit.
2. According to elderly informants in Western Kukwe, Mwakaleli and some central chiefdoms, and also the evidence of old village sites.

my earlier labour migration enquiries in the Highlands, the village as a close residential unit is breaking up as the people are increasingly adopting the more common East African pattern of each family building its own homestead in its own land-holding. These northern Nyakyusa say that they must have their coffee plots next to their homesteads for the sake of continuous supervision, and that this is impossible (which is true enough) where men live close together in compact villages. Again, coffee plots, with their standing, permanent trees, have become a valuable item of inheritance; sons lose no opportunity of taking them irrespective of the locations of their coevals or of the identity of their immediate neighbours. The values of land, cash-crops and material progress are placed much higher than the traditional values of coevality; indeed, such traditional values are largely inconsistent with modern wants and aspirations.

Thus the Nyakyusa age-village has become almost obsolete and it would seem that it must inevitably vanish altogether even in the remaining conservative areas (e.g., in the east). Furthermore, its disappearance is leading to a distinct divergence between the Lake Plains Nyakyusa and those of the Highlands. How far this divergence will become permanent and basically significant cannot be foreseen as yet in this early stage. Clearly the compact village is best fitted to an arable economy of rice cultivation in the Lake Plains, and at least until there is further agricultural change it will persist as a most important social group.

Nevertheless, with its enhanced exclusiveness and relative social isolation and with renewed rivalry with its neighbours, the Lake Plains village is scarcely conducive to the encouragement of agricultural and economic development. Neither is it anything but harmful towards contemporary efforts in the politico-administrative sphere to reduce parochialism and to foster a sense of unity and co-operation beyond the village and the petty traditional chiefdoms. Whilst supervisory control of the land through the headman is in general excellent, reasonable and readily understandable to the people, yet the excess of restrictiveness, the competitive scrambling for vacated holdings and the jealous fears are surely more than merely unfortunate. There needs to be some modification to loosen the over-tight strings of village corporate ownership, to regularise the transfer of vacated holdings and to lessen the fears of village against village. These points are taken up again in Chapter V.

Cattle and Pastoral Requirements

Unfortunately, no great accuracy can be presumed for the Rungwe District cattle censuses, but the available figures are summarised in Table VI.

TABLE VI
NYAKYUSA CATTLE

	1955				1951	
	No. of cattle	Acres per beast	Cattle per person	Cattle per family of 5	No. of cattle	Acres per beast
Lake Plains	31,418	4.1	0.5	2.5	26,822	5.2
Central Region ..	19,380	7.1	0.4	2	19,160	7.2
N.E. Highlands ..	19,095	7.4	0.4	2	17,165	8.4
N.W. Highlands ..	22,974	8.0	0.4	2	16,855	10.9
Total:						
Nyakyusa.. ..	92,867	6.4	0.4	2	80,002	7.2

The indicated increase in the numbers of cattle may well be attributable only to improved census enumeration by the Veterinary Department.

Although 6.4 acres per head of cattle for all Nyakyusa country, and even 4.1 acres in the Lake Plains, might seem to be adequate in a country so

34

well covered with vegetation and with so reliable and plentiful a rainfall, yet, of course, the actual pasturage available is very considerably less as so much of the land is taken for arable and building purposes. There is in practice a most acute shortage of grazing land everywhere, except in certain parts of the north-west Highlands (Ukukwe). This shortage is most critical during the wet season, for at other times of the year the herds are able to graze over the arable fields, where herbage grows exceptionally rapidly after harvest as a result of the high rainfall.

Traditionally, each village had a roughly demarcated area of common pasturage which was not, and could not be, used for arable purposes. With the increased demand for arable land, this commonage has almost everywhere in the Lake Plains been gradually whittled away for permanent arable holdings. Headmen who control these pastures, and many of their chiefs too, are much worried about this process, about the break with tradition and the modern pastoral difficulties; but arable needs are given priority over grazing and the practice continues. In the flood plains, the higher-density regions, common pasturage has by now almost disappeared altogether. The little which remains is largely unusable for cultivation, consisting of infertile or badly drained areas – often the sandy, coastal strips covered with dense thicket and tall sedges which provide very little useful grazing. During the dry season, after the paddy harvest, the situation is fair, but during the cultivation season pasturage is entirely inadequate, and in addition the cattle are compelled to live and graze in extremely arduous conditions of standing water, mud, mosquitoes and flies. They do not obtain enough food then and they lose condition badly. There are many deaths from exhaustion, near-starvation and disease, and this affects the immature stock particularly. Only by obstinate tenacity on the part of both man and beast can the herds be retained at all. There is no tradition of stall-feeding and so far the Nyakyusa have refused to adopt this measure of alleviation.

Yet, as the Nyakyusa are quick to point out, each family has only a few cattle. Most families have a cow or two, and the average is only about two to three head per family – cf. Table VI, page 34. Owners of large herds are relatively few, and herds of more than ten cattle in a single family are very uncommon. Although the cattle population is too great for the pasture resources now available, yet the animals are fairly evenly and thinly distributed amongst the dense human population. Goats and sheep are few – about 600 altogether – in the Lake Plains and of no significance. It is important to note that here we do not have a situation of large herds which might be reduced by some form of culling.

Cattle are held in high esteem by all Nyakyusa as a source of valued milk for the daily diet, as the means to marriage (in bridewealth), as a store of capital, as a symbol of prestige and as an essential element in important ceremonial activity. This kind of value system needs no emphasis here as it is common to much of Eastern Africa, but it may be noted that one of the principle uses of the large sums of money saved from wages in mining employment (labour migration)[1] and from the profits of cash-cropping at home is in the purchase of cattle. It is thought that money is best invested, saved and used in that way, once immediate material needs have been met.

Even with the high proportion of deaths from disease and the appalling conditions of the wet season, there are indications that the numbers of cattle are not decreasing and there may well be local increases. Apart from natural increase, there is fairly heavy buying from the Ndali people to the north-west in Rungwe District, and also from farther afield in Northern Nyasaland, and in Nyamwanga and Fipa tribal areas (albeit illicitly).

---

1. During the course of my earlier labour migration enquiries men would usually estimate their savings for me, when completing routine questionnaires, by the number of cattle they could buy.

Whereas in the Highland and Central regions the large numbers of cattle – in relation, that is, to the available pasture resources – are causing over-grazing and soil erosion, particularly in the hilly areas so often nowadays relegated to pasturage, on the other hand in the flood plains there does not appear, at least to the layman, to have been any serious effects on the land. The natural manuring of the paddy fields in the dry season is advantageous. In the Lake Plains it is the cattle rather than the land which suffer, but so far the Nyakyusa have done virtually nothing to meet the new conditions, other than to complain bitterly and fruitlessly.

The Young Men: Land Shortage and Labour Migration

The younger Nyakyusa men find increasing difficulty in obtaining arable land now that there are no longer vacant areas to be taken up, and the older men are no longer prepared to cede their land rights in favour of the younger generation, as they traditionally did. When occasional fields are left vacant, the young men must take their turn with their elders, who themselves are so chronically short of land – and the headmen commonly favour the older villagers with families as against the younger men. This means that in the high-density regions the majority of men under the age of about 30 years have little or no arable land, nor can they hope for it until the deaths of their fathers. In the congested village sites even their banana plots may be smaller than is desirable for the provision of the staple food.

The young man, then, is compelled to remain dependent on his father's and elder brother's holding; indeed, headmen often justify their refusals to allocate plots to young men on the express grounds that the latter must share their elders' fields. Thus the valued independence of the young Nyakyusa is severely restricted and it seems that tensions and difficulties are beginning to arise between fathers and sons, and between brothers, because of this. Sons are blamed for not doing their fair share in the family cultivation; fathers are blamed for giving their sons inadequate shares in crops and crop incomes. It will be remembered that one of the fundamental principles underlying Nyakyusa society and its age-village organisation is the spatial segregation of parents and children (cf. page 22). Now they are inevitably being put into competition with one another over inadequate fields in a single holding.

The young men are severely restricted, if not altogether cut off, from the opportunity to cultivate paddy in their own fields and thus to earn their incomes at home, for paddy-growing is the only way of earning a living in the Lake Plains. Yet it is these younger men whose money demand is greatest; to buy clothing, bicycles and other store-goods, and to buy cattle for marriage payments. They are therefore strongly attracted by the ready opportunities for taking up wage-labour abroad, in the mines of the Rhodesias and South Africa where wages are high (see Gulliver, 1957).

With the best will in the world, when, as in the very high-density region, the average holding is little more than an acre and a half – when, that is, the older men themselves desire larger acreages for their own cultivation needs – it is not possible for a father to allow his son to take large shares in his fields. In some cases a father does give outright to his adult sons strips of his holding, but plots so provided are necessarily small. Quite as frequently a father does not consider it possible to break up his holding in his own life-time, and sons are expected to assist in the common cultivation and to continue merely to be given a share in the family proceeds at harvest. It is not surprising, therefore, that very large numbers of young men from the Lake Plains migrate abroad to work. Only about one man in 20 has not been away at all before the age of about 25 years. Much higher proportions of men and larger numbers absolutely are temporarily absent from the Lake

36

Plains than from any other Nyakyusa area. In the high-density regions, the proportion of young men away at any one time is about 50 per cent. on the average and the proportion has risen concomitantly with the increasing scarcity of land.

It is not, of course, suggested that land shortage is the only factor responsible for contemporary labour migration amongst the Nyakyusa. Elsewhere (*loc. cit.*) I have drawn attention to the very high wages, the increased opportunity to obtain outside employment, the development of transport services and the intensification of recruiting, together with the general desire of the people to gain a higher standard of living as they more thoroughly embrace the new money economy. In fact, wage-labour in the mines is more profitable than growing paddy at home under current agricultural practice, even were land more easily available. Nevertheless, more young men do leave their homes in the Lake Plains than elsewhere in the country, and there is a rough correlation between land availability and the degree of labour migration, which seems to indicate that where men can obtain more land they tend to seek their money incomes at home. The Nyakyusa themselves, with an intensity of tribal patriotism, say that they much prefer to remain at home if they can earn their money there, even if they earn rather less than they might obtain abroad; but, say the young men, it is impossible to earn anything like sufficient when the fields are unobtainable in which to cultivate the cash-crop.

The data which I have been able to collect are summarised in Table VII. Young men are defined here as those under about 30 years old.

TABLE VII

YOUNG MEN: LAND HOLDING AND LABOUR MIGRATION

Village and chiefdom	Young men having own paddy field	Young men away at work	Average holding of:	
			Young men who own land	Older men in same village
1. Very high density region				
Mpunguti Mwakipesile ..	17%	53%	0.5 acres	1.9 acres
Kapugi Koroso	25%	54%	0.75 acres	1.5 acres
Ndobo Mwakyusa ..	28%	51%	—	—
2. High density region				
Ikolo Mwakyusa ..	37%	47%	1.6 acres	3.7 acres
Kapugi Mwamasangula	52%	39%	1.25 acres	4.5 acres

There are some young men who have small food-crop plots but no paddy field, but I have chosen to correlate labour migration with paddy cultivation because these are almost the only alternative ways of earning money today, and the people themselves recognise the fact. The number of samples is too small, but the general inference seems to be quite clear nonetheless. My own conclusions in this matter were, however, arrived at independently of these figures, which were only obtained for corroboration. The evidence of the people themselves and their obvious difficulties of earning money at home were overwhelming.

If anything is required to underline the current land shortage and to illustrate the small size of the average holding, it surely lies in the existence of villages in which only about one quarter of the young men have their own paddy fields, and in which the average holding of this minority amounts to less than an acre.

Only in the low-density region can the young men obtain the fields they require. There, as they did traditionally, the young adult sons continue to assist their fathers in the heavier labour in the fields, but gradually before marriage they accumulate and extend their own holdings and so achieve economic independence. Elsewhere in the Lake Plains this process is taking much longer and indeed it now very frequently awaits inheritance at the death of the father. The old principle that every man had the right to arable land applied no less strongly to the young men, married or bachelors. Today most headmen will refuse to entertain the applications of young bachelors for land, and in this they merely represent general public opinion. But many young husbands likewise cannot obtain land, or only an insufficient amount.

Consequently, the following case-history, which I recorded for one young man, is not unusual. In 1955 he lived in the Mlangali young-men's hamlet, attached to Mpunguti village in Mwakipesile's chiefdom, where his father lives. He was about 27 years old and had a wife and one child. Twice he had been to work in the mines and from the profits of this employment he had completed his bridewealth payment and had bought, in addition, three cattle, a bicycle and some good clothing. He thought he would probably go away again. Behind his house his wife had about 300 square yards of bananas and there was a tiny patch of cassava. This man had no other land, but he assisted in the heavy labour on his father's holding (about 1.7 acres in all) and by family convention he normally took for his own use the paddy crop of a small strip there; he insisted, however, that he had not been given this strip outright and that it remained at his father's pleasure. He had an unmarried half-brother about 22 years old who had not obtained even that concession at the time. Their father was about 55 years old and had two other sons who were still boys. The young man himself had been refused an allocation of land by the headman on the grounds that (as the headman well knew) he had the use of this strip of his father's land, and also because, as the eldest son, he would be the principal heir on his father's death. He was clearly worried about his future, for he did not wish to go abroad again and leave his wife and child; but he did not see how he could stay at home without seriously lowering his standard of living to little above subsistence level.

I quote this brief case-history not necessarily as typical – though I think it probably is – but as an actual illustration of the present state of affairs as they affect an individual.

The Modern "Chief" and the Land

Most of the traditional chiefs, *abanyafyale*, have been recognised and salaried under the Native Authority, and they are officially referred to today as *abatwa* (s. *ntwa*). Some of the smallest chiefdoms have been absorbed administratively by their larger neighbours, and, although they are still recognised by the people, their *abanyafyale* have lost very much of their earlier prestige and authority. In the Lake Plains the modern chiefdoms are often rather larger than is usual amongst the Nyakyusa,[1] but they are, of course, small in comparison with the size of most African chiefdoms in Tanganyika.

The slightness of the traditional authority of the chief in land matters has already been noted (pages 7-8) and in general this still holds. In European times, however, the recognised chiefs have been given an increased authority and prestige as the local intermediaries between Government and people, and until recent years they were almost the only local instruments of the Government amongst the Nyakyusa. They have been backed by the all-powerful European, who preferred to deal with single, recognised individuals thought to have prime authority in a locality, and the European officer has been encouraged in this notion by an over-enthusiastic policy of indirect rule. Such chiefs were able to assume a degree of power well beyond the traditional limits, and to aggrandize themselves thereby. The ordinary commoner was never quite sure how far his chief was individually claiming more than he

---

1. On the numerical sizes of chiefdoms see supra, page 6.

had authority to claim, or how far the Central Government was permitting or even compelling him to use new powers. Part of this novel power has, not unnaturally, been used to take over land-control responsibilities to which the chief has no traditional tribal right, and it has led to the claims, sometimes heard in the Courts and upheld in the District Commissioner's Appeal Court, that chiefs are the sole, traditional and rightful land authorities. It has led to chiefs assuming, or trying to assume, land allocation and supervisory powers which hitherto were the close right only of the village headmen.

Thus some chiefs have declared that they alone, or at least primarily, have allocatory powers over formerly uncultivated tracts which are relatively distant from the villages and which have now become valuable as paddy fields. Others have come to claim rights of interference in village land affairs, even within the long-established village areas. By the undefined threat of their alleged Government support, by taking advantage of new conditions, they have not infrequently "got away with it". They have insisted that their own nominees be allocated vacant holdings; they have gone over the heads of village headmen and made public their opinion as to who, amongst numbers of aspirants, should receive land in villages; they have insisted that headmen should consult them on the details of allocation. The desire for power and further prestige is one impulse behind this development. Sometimes the chiefs, better educated than many of their headmen, are able to understand the modern land situation better and are impatient of their headmen's conservatism and procrastination. Another factor is the potential profit which may accrue as land becomes scarce and thus a valuable commodity, and this became particularly important when the rush developed to take up the formerly vacant lands for paddy cultivation. Gifts in money and kind became common in return for preferential treatment for the donors. These lands are now all allocated and held by someone, but the chiefs have been reluctant to relinquish their new-found authority.

These remarks do not apply to all the chiefs: some have been notably content to use their influence through the traditional system by judicious co-operation with their headmen. Some, too, have been too imperceptive to bother to take action at all. Again, some have been forestalled by strong village headmen who would not allow any diminution of their own status and rights. In some of the fomerly vacant lands where no headman could reasonably claim traditional jurisdiction, the operations of the chiefs have probably been beneficial in reducing chaotic land-grabbing and jealous rivalry; once, however, these lands are brought under cultivation there seems to be a good case for their inclusion within the normal Nyakyusa land-control system. The continued existence of a supra-headman authority does not necessarily lead to stability or improved control. Certainly it is not in keeping with the people's values and institutions.

For these changes Government must clearly bear some responsibility and often also the blame for indirectly causing alterations in native land law and custom by some administrative attitude or ruling in a related sphere. There has been a good deal of well-intentioned insistence on determining and strengthening the "Land Authority" in tribal areas in the interests of stability and efficiency. In Rungwe District the facile claims of Nyakyusa chiefs have been only too readily accepted without question. In fact the traditional *umalafyale*, chief, only represented his chiefdom as a unit, and his lack of real power corresponded to the lack of cohesion within the chiefdom. The notion of a supreme "Land Authority" is largely incorrect for the Nyakyusa. In a theoretical sense we may perhaps say that the total land of a chiefdom was and is owned by all of the people in that chiefdom – chief, headmen and villagers; and therefore we may perhaps categorise the chief, the single individual representing the group as a whole, as the "land-owner." To do this is however, seriously to strain the facts and values beyond what the average Nyakusa would understand or allow. The chief does not, as we have seen, allocate land either to villages as individual units or to the villagers separately; new, traditional villages obtained their land by allocation from the old headmen, and individual villagers were and are allocated their holdings by their own headman. The chief can act as arbitrator between villagers and villages, but his decisions have been notoriously difficult to enforce. Undoubtedly commoners resent the attempts by their chief to interfere in their own village affairs.

Now it may, of course, be desirable to widen and thus facilitate the scope of land authority, allocatory responsibility and equitable supervision, especially in the interests of a developing cash economy in a situation of a critical shortage of land. But if this significant change in native land law is to be introduced, it should surely be as a result of a proper appreciation of the facts and the existing law, and it must be in conformity with the interests and desires of the people themselves. It ought not to be a gradual sliding into a new situation as a result of other factors – as a by-product of local government development, for example, or as a matter of administrative convenience unsupported by real understanding. To make the chiefs the executive agents of the local government system does not necessarily mean – or it should not – that they should be passively allowed to usurp the land allocation powers of their headmen. Further, in view of modern Territorial policy aimed at bringing the people and their village leaders into the local government system, it seems perhaps unwise that at the same time chiefs should be allowed to assert non-traditional, autocratic land powers which are resented by villagers and headmen, and which may do little to improve the already difficult situation. When the additional powers of the chiefs are used at least partly, if not mainly, for self-aggrandizement or for personal profit, then it is a trend which needs to be strictly curtailed and controlled.

CHAPTER V

CONCLUSIONS AND SUGGESTIONS

Briefly to summarise the contemporary land situation: in the Lake Plains it may be said that in the main the traditional land tenure system and land law still continue as the basis of native land holding today. The essential feature in recent years has been the acute land shortage in relation to arable needs under the current system of agriculture. Village unity and village exclusiveness have been increased and so also has the authority of the village headman in his control and allocation of land rights. Security of tenure has been strengthened, if anything, and one of the most important methods of obtaining land is now by inheritance. The new law establishing inheritance from father to sons, whilst generally acceptable to the people, is producing a number of civil suits which form the greatest proportion of the more important land cases before the local courts.

The shortage of land is principally the result of increased demands for paddy (i.e. cash crop) cultivation, although the population appears to be increasing slowly. In the high density regions almost all men have considerably less land than they could cultivate, especially under the impetus of the ox-plough, with the developing desires for money income. In the low density region of the low foothills there is still some vacant or partly utilised land, though of very inferior quality for paddy cultivation. The shortage hits the younger men severely, and many of them cannot obtain land at all until the death or senility of their fathers. Fragmentation and dispersion of holdings is rapidly becoming serious and without check.

The first question which arises is whether anything can be done to ease the pressure of population on the country by making more land available, or by making its distribution more equitable.

The thinly populated parts of the northern region of the Lake Plains offer a meagre solution only, for the country is raised above the level of the flood plains and is often broken and hilly. Fertility is low, erosion is a constant danger and the paddy yield (if obtainable at all) is poor. Nyakyusa from the densely populated areas to south and east are therefore most unwilling to move there. In any case the available land, which remains safely and economically open to cultivation, is filling up fairly quickly – mainly by immigration. Certainly I do not think that it can supply sufficient space to meet modern needs. There is, however, no reason why immigrants should make a difficult situation worse, and therefore it is suggested that further immigration from outside the Lake Plains should be carefully controlled if not altogether prevented. Indubitably outsiders (almost entirely Nyakyusa from the Highlands) who hold land without permanent residence should be prohibited and their holdings reallocated to local inhabitants.

As I have already indicated (page 17), I do not think that the problem of men who hold unusually large acreages is particularly serious. Such large holdings are relatively few and will be inevitably split up by inheritance on the deaths of the present occupiers.

In the flood plains proper there is, as far as I am aware, extremely little new land which could be brought under cultivation. Mechanical assistance in the clearance of dense reed thicket[1] and in drainage schemes would produce

---

1. These areas of thicket are heavily inundated in the wet season but, if cleared, could be used for a dry season crop.

some more land. How much could be made cultivable is beyond my appraisal, but it would be of valuable local assistance and ought not to be neglected. It does not, on the other hand, appear practicable to decrease further the amount of land used for building and village sites – the people themselves have already done this to some extent, and increased congestion in the villages would probably be undesirable on medical grounds.

There remain the local cases where part or all of a holding is not used (excluding genuine fallowing). An old man, or one who has for some reason lost the labour of his wives or sons, is sometimes unable to cultivate the whole of his fields. This is not common, or if it occurs the occupier is usually approached by his kinsmen, friends and neighbours for a loan or gift. Occasionally such land does remain relatively unutilised and the occupier refuses to release it even at the request of the headman. There is some feeling in the Lake Plains over this matter, and some men have suggested openly that such unused land should compulsorily revert to the village to be re-allocated by the headman.[1] Unless there is overwhelming demand for a new ruling here it would seem not to be a practicable policy and would only weaken security of land-holding and further increase the already over-exaggerated communal claim of the village. It would, of course, be difficult to assess when in fact a man had more land than he could or would cultivate, and it might easily lead to injustice if chiefs or headmen were given powers (however restricted) to interfere in a man's holding. Nevertheless headmen might be encouraged to keep a close watch on unused fields in their villages and to bring pressure to bear either to persuade the occupier to increase his efforts or to make temporary, witnessed loans to a neighbour.

In some cases land is left unused for a period whilst a man is away from home – usually while he is away at work. Where his absence is brief, little can or needs to be done, and already under Nyakyusa law the headman may authorise another villager to cultivate the fields on a year to year tenure: the absentee re-entering his holding on return. Occasionally, however, a young man may, for example, inherit land but then leave it for a number of years whilst he migrates to work in the mines. There is no adequate ruling as to the number of years' absence which should elapse before the absentee forfeits his land as an assumed permanent emigrant from the village. Head-men are reluctant to reallocate unused land for fear of the obvious legal and social difficulties should the absentee return, although some headmen are more hasty than others in this matter. Neighbours are often reluctant to borrow the land for fear of losing their opportunity of an outright allocation else-where in the village in the meantime. In some cases I saw fields which had lain unused for more than four years for these reasons. Like the unused portions of an old man's holding, these few cases arouse a good deal of land-hungry indignation, beyond their real importance in fact. Nevertheless some limit to the period of absence might well be introduced so that at least headmen know what their authority is in this matter, and so that men not prepared to work the land shall not be able to retain it indefinitely, It may be noted that the average length of absence of men in migratory labour is 18-24 months. A period of three years' continuous absence, at least without special cause, might perhaps be taken to indicate the automatic abdication of right of tenure.

If more land cannot be made available – or only relatively little – the obvious solution is a more intensive and profitable use of the existing re-sources. The Agricultural Department has long urged this policy and is attempting to put it into effect, pointing out the relatively inferior yields of paddy in the Lake Plains because of poor techniques and inefficient effort.

---

1. Significantly enough, one of the men to bring this suggestion to my notice was the Nyakyusa Senior Agricultural Instructor in the Lake Plains.

This is not the province of the Sociologist, and all that can be said here is that it seems the most practical and valuable policy that could be adopted: it should be made the chief line of attack on contemporary problems. Unfortunately the Nyakyusa do not appreciate the value of this sort of solution – at least not yet – and therefore they are not inclined to learn and to increase their efforts and to change their practices in the fields. They have not yet rid themselves of the notion that increased production of crops and thus increased profits from agriculture are correlated only with increased holdings. In view of the critical land shortage a crucial change of attitude and understanding is required. The Nyakyusa must learn that increased production and higher profits can come from new and more efficient techniques – i.e. intensive cultivation. They must also learn what is so difficult for the African, that quality of production is no less important than quantity and that therefore cash incomes and standards of living can be raised by improving the standard of crops to be sold. Indeed, with a tendency for world agricultural prices to fall due to increasing supply, quality of produce is of the greatest importance. This is notably so in the case of rice. Tanganyika African rice is reckoned as of lower quality than that from South-east Asia, which therefore commands not only the better price but also the main share of the keenly competitive market. But it is a difficult idea for the Nyakyusa to grasp. It seems obvious to them, inheriting attitudes of a former subsistence age, that three poor cattle are better than two good ones – and in fact so they were in the hazardous time of their grandfathers. Cash crop production is based on the same premise, but it cannot hold in a modern cash economy and in dealings with world markets.

If, however, the present land shortage continues unchecked by the successful introduction of new attitudes, ideas and techniques there may well be serious social and political repercussions in the not too distant future. Current schemes of tribal development will surely be rendered futile if economic activity is restricted and if land discontent is allowed to become important.

A second agricultural policy, and one of which less is heard, would be to stop the present dangerous monoculture – the persistence with paddy alone – and to attempt on a large scale to introduce second and third cash crops, particularly such crops as require intensive cultivation on small acreages. This may be forced on the people in any case if the gloomy prognostications of world rice prices are borne out in the next few years. Such a development would allow of a more stable economy and a more balanced agriculture, in addition to assisting towards a reduction of land difficulties. Experiments on a small scale in robusta coffee, palm oil and other crops have already been started by the Agricultural Department but, at least from the layman's point of view, they need priority in finance, attention and effort as a main part of an agricultural programme for the Lake Plains.

In the time available for my investigations it was not possible to enquire with sufficient care into the details and exact procedure of Nyakyusa land law (c.f. page 3) and therefore I am reluctant to suggest any drastic changes. The new inheritance law (page 21) is a step in the right direction and is clearly in keeping with modern trends, but it is suggested that its detailed operation on the ground and in the courts should be studied by the Native Authority and the Administration in order to attempt to define its meaning more clearly and to reduce the number of disputes. In order to check fragmentation before it has gone too far, it should be considered whether some minimum limit might not be imposed on the size of fields. Voluntary schemes for the consolidation of holdings, which have achieved some success elsewhere in Africa, might also be considered. These would be particularly valuable in the flood plains paddy fields where the ox-plough is in general use today. The general advantages of consolidation require no exposition here.

In view of the domestic, economic and social importance of cattle to the Nyakyusa and their potential value in a mixed intensive economy, and also in view of the fact that cattle are widely held in very small numbers by individual families, it is suggested that further and more urgent attempts be made to encourage stall-feeding, especially during the wet season. It is realised that past efforts in this matter have failed, and therefore a thorough-going scheme of propaganda and demonstration work is needed. Small fodder crops might be grown in the dry season and there is always plenty of banana fodder as makeweight.

The problem of the landless young men is likely to remain very difficult (see pages 36ff). It has to be remembered of course, that as they get older men do acquire land gradually. Nevertheless the proportion of landless, or virtually landless, men is high and is apparently increasing. The large-scale, post-war labour migration to the Rhodesias and South Africa is undoubtedly one of the more important results of land shortage and economic difficulty, and it is a valuable safety valve. As I have written elsewhere: "The serious and increasing land shortage amongst the Nyakyusa raises real doubts if there is any policy at all which can keep the men at home when there is not enough land for them – for the sake of both economic and general social stability it might be preferable in the long run if the continued pressure on the land resources were released by a degree of permanent emigration."[1] Since writing that and during the course of my land investigations I have only become more convinced of its rightness. I would now go so far as to say that Nyakyusa men should be encouraged to go abroad to work and even to become permanent wage-labourers in the industries and areas which demand labour and offer a higher standard of living. If the Nyakyusa are not to be seriously retarded in their home economic development, based as it must be on agriculture (i.e. on the land), the excess population must find an outlet elsewhere.

The general tendency towards greatly increased exclusiveness in the Nyakyusa village, involving renewed emphasis on the principle of land-holding only by residence and the forfeiture of a holding when changing residence, raises wider issues the future significance of which is not easily seen, especially by the Nyakyusa themselves. This narrow village parochialism does little to meet the increasingly difficult problem of land shortage, whilst the isolation it fosters is the antithesis of the wider outlook required by a developing society in a world money economy. I am fully aware of the strong native sentiment attached to the village and to village independence, but this was in fact diminishing in earlier European times before the new land scarcity set in (see pages 29-30). I do not think that this village system and the complex of attitudes and values it fosters is adequate to provide for the future – a future which the Nyakyusa do not yet clearly foresee. With some deference, therefore, I offer the following suggestion: a man who already has a holding should be able to retain it when he moves to live in another village. If his new home is too far away for the continued cultivation of all or part of the holding, or for any other valid reason, he should be able to sell or give it to anyone he wishes. Such gift or sale could be supervised by the headman of the village in which the holding lies. It might well, at first at any rate, be limited to a member of the same village, either an established villager or another man who is willing to come and live there. I think it important that disposal should be outright and not on leasehold terms, for the latter would most propably engender further complications and uncertainty of tenure, which must be avoided.

1. Gulliver, P. H.: *A Report on the Migration of African Workers to the South from the Southern Highlands Province, with special reference to the Nyakyusa of Rungwe District.* Provincial Administration, Tanganyika, 1955, page A21.

Thus men wishing to move could seek to obtain, that is to buy, a holding from another man living in a village to which he is willing to move; a man leaving a village could either retain his holding in cultivation or obtain some compensation for the loss of his holding there. It is not likely that this would produce a rush of land sales, for only a relatively few men would wish to relinquish their holdings. It would, however, facilitate freer movement between villages. Secondly, it would assist younger men to obtain holdings when they have earned and saved money at work.[1] Thirdly, it would assist profit-making cultivators to enlarge their holdings. Fourthly, it would help to bring to the Nyakyusa a realisation of the implications of the new money economy which they have inevitably and irrevocably entered, and it would demonstrate the value of holdings in relation to other commodities and activities. This kind of system would allow the village to retain much of its valued unity and control whilst reducing its excessive and potentially harmful exclusiveness. Such disposals of land, especially if by money sale, could be performed before the headman and other reliable village witnesses and they could be registered formally at the local court. There would need also to be some ruling limiting the maximum size of holdings (to prevent excessive buying) and preventing alienation to Africans from outside the Lake Plains. In this matter the village headman would probably be the executive authority.

Although the suggestion could be introduced simply as a scheme enabling the buying and selling of land, I am here more concerned with the problem of freer movement and the limitation of the reversionary rights of the headman on behalf of the village, whilst retaining his useful controls. A more general recognition of the economic value of land would probably follow, and if it proved practicable and useful, an extended and refined scheme could be introduced later.

My suggestions are, then, as follows:—

1. (a) an immediate restriction of immigration into the Lake Plains from whatever origin, and the encouragement of the movement of people from the congested areas into the lightly populated areas, accompanied by local development programmes there;

(b) the consideration of the practicability of drainage and thicket clearance schemes in order to make more land available;

(c) the absolute abolition of land-holding by non-residents and the reallocation through the local headmen of land so held to local inhabitants;

(d) the sympathetic encouragement of village headmen to watch unused portions of villagers' holdings with a view to their voluntary and temporary reallocation to neighbours in need.

2. (a) a detailed enquiry into the operation and administration of the new inheritance law, with a view to improving its details;

(b) an enquiry into the possibility of imposing a minimum limit on the size of holdings and plots;

(c) the introduction of local, voluntary schemes for the consolidation of holdings.

3. Covering the whole field of Nyakyusa land problems must necessarily be a progressive agricultural programme aimed, firstly, at a more intensive and a more efficient use of the land by improved cultivation methods, and, secondly, the abolition of monoculture by the introduction of other cash crops. This is, of course, the policy of the Agricultural Department, but it needs more urgent application despite the obvious difficulties raised.

Stall-feeding of cattle, especially in the wet season, would assist to improve the living conditions of the herds and to increase their domestic and economic value.

---

1. It would also provide an alternative cash investment to the present purchase of cattle.

45

4. The safety valve of labour migration should not be closed and young Nyakyusa should be encouraged to go away to work whilst wages abroad are relatively high.

5. Finally, with a view to the future as well as the present, it is suggested that an individual's land-holding should be at his own disposal, and, if desired, by money sale. Purchasers should, at first anyway, be limited to members of the village where the holding lies or to men willing to settle there.

These recommendations are to be taken only as a suggested programme for administrative consideration. No attempt can be made here to lay down the details of future policy, for that is the function and responsibility of administrators and technical officers, African and European, and not of the Sociologist.

The Sociologist could, however, with profit participate in the discussions and work preparatory to the development of a satisfactory programme. It is essential that a complete programme be arranged and executed to tackle all or most of the problems concerning the land, economics and agriculture. Tinkering with different aspects here and there is likely to be unfruitful and is unlikely to command the propaganda and drive of a comprehensive scheme. Such a planned scheme should be able to catch the imagination and support of the people themselves, especially if they and their leaders can be brought to see the reasons for it and the value it may bring.

Bibliography

Throughout the essay the following works of reference are given in brief form only:—

Wilson, G. (1938)   – *The Land Rights of Individuals Among the Nyakyusa*, Rhodes-Livingstone Paper, No. 1.

Wilson, M. (1950)   – "Nyakyusa Kinship," in *African Systems of Kinship and Marriage*, ed. A. R. Radcliffe-Brown and Daryll Forde, International African Institute, London.

Wilson, M. (1951)   – *Good Company: a Study of Nyakusa Age-villages*, International African Institute, London.

Gulliver, P. H. (1957) – "Nyakyusa Labour Migration," *Rhodes-Livingstone Journal*, No. XXI, pp. 32-63.

N.B. In Wilson, M. (1951) there is a full bibliography of works dealing with the Nyakyusa.

THE 1957 POPULATION CENSUS

Since this Report was originally written there has been a new census of the African population in Tanganyika. This took place in August, 1957, and the first official results have been published by the East African Statistical Department in *Tanganyika African Population Census, 1957. Analysis by sex and age for Province, District and Territorial Census Areas,* March, 1958.

In this note are given these latest data relevant to the subject matter of this report. The following Table is set out in the same form as Table I on page 12 in which my original estimates were given. As in that Table, so here, no account is taken of unusable land such as swamp, steep slopes, thicket, etc., in the calculation of densities and available acreages.

NYAKYUSA POPULATION

	1948 Population	1957 Population	Density per sq. mile	Acres per family of 5	Average annual increase 1948-57
Lake Plains ..	55,700	66,513	320	10.0	2.0%
Central Region ..	48,500	48,305	223	14.3	0.0%
N. W. Highlands	53,200	65,075	226	14.2	2.3%
N. E. Highlands ..	40,300	44,697	203	15.8	1.2%
NYAKYUSA in tribal area ..	197,700	224,590	241	13.3	1.4%

N.B. There are some members of other tribes in the Nyakyusa tribal area who cannot be excluded from these figures.

Assuming that in 1957 there were about 6,000 men temporarily absent from their homes in the Lake Plains but who remained dependent on the land resources of that region, then the following estimate may be made:—

Lake Plains – persons resident at home and temporarily abroad:—

58,700	72,513	349	9.2

The changes in population during this nine-year period, in so far as they are indicated by the results of these two censuses, differ a little from what was suggested in Chapter III. Improved enumeration may well account for some of the increase; but, apart from such mechanical errors, it is clear that there has been a relatively large increase of population in the Lake Plains, and in the North-Western Highlands. I suggest that the natural increase in the Lake Plains has been 1-1½ per cent. a year, and the remaining increase has come from immigration (cf. pages 18 ff). The same is probably true for the North-Western Highlands where immigration has occurred because some land remained in that region which could still be taken up (unlike other parts of the country). It is noteworthy that the population of the relatively poor Central Region, which has no cash crop and easily eroded land, has remained the same at the end of the period. Undoubtedly there has been emigration from this region to the Lake Plains and the North-Western Highlands.

As far as this report is concerned, the population has been increasing more rapidly and the density is greater than my original figures indicated. I am inclined to think now that the population of the "very high density" region of the Lake Plains (page 16) must be well over 500 people per square mile – probably up to 600 people per square mile. Pressure on the land is, therefore, more acute than I reported, and the pressure on the social system of the Nyakyusa is similarly greater. This does not affect the main analysis and argument of the report.

May, 1958.